CULTIVATING
THE MIND

CULTIVATING THE MIND

A Path Toward Enlightenment

KIM JAE WOONG

YongHwa

About the Author

Born in 1942, Dharma Master Kim Jae Woong spent his childhood in Pohang in the southeast of Korea. In 1964, he met Master Baek Sung Wook and began to study and practice the Dharma under his guidance. For seven years and six months, he underwent a rigorous period of spiritual training at Sosa Monastery. He awakened to deep reverence and wisdom at the monastery, and resolved to dedicate his entire life to serving Buddha and the Dharma. He became a celibate practitioner and led a simple and frugal life, living in a tiny room and eating only twice a day. Since 1973, he has led the Diamond Sutra Recitation Group, establishing two monasteries for full-time practitioners and fifteen Dharma halls for lay practitioners in Korea, Germany, UK and the USA. Following the principle of not relying on donations or offerings, Master Kim and his students earn their own living by farming and making traditional foods such as soy sauce, soybean paste, sesame oil, and perilla oil. The Diamond Sutra Recitation Group has donated more than 600,000 copies of the Diamond Sutra to temples, schools, and military bases, greatly contributing to the study and practice of the Diamond Sutra nationwide. Since 1997, the Group has donated ten thousand dollars annually to international charity organizations. Since 2005, it has run the Korean Spirit and Culture Promotion Project. As part of this project, the group has published books on Korean historical figures and cultural heritage, and distributed 710,000 copies free of charge. Master Kim's other writings include *Polishing the Diamond Enlightening the Mind* (Korean and English), *Surrender That Mind* (Korean), and *Exert The Mind Without Attachment* (Korean).

PREFACE

When you face difficulties in life, or when you are deeply angered by something, how do you govern the mind? How do you tame the body that expresses itself through words and actions?

As you hold back, restrain yourself, endure, and cultivate the mind by practicing humility and surrendering, a path will open before your eyes. Someone who continues such practice in daily life will become a truly able person.

When our lives are over and we depart from this world, we leave behind a record of our actions and also take a copy of this record with us. This record contains all of the sins we have committed, the good deeds and acts of merit we have performed, and the extent to which we have cultivated the mind. How therefore should we live each day of our lives?

This book is a selection of public lectures I have given on the teachings of the Diamond Sutra. Since 1998, with the help of Buddhist military chaplain Kim Ung, our group has donated over 1.6 million pocket-sized copies of this book to the Korea Army Training Center in Nonsan and other military bases. Many servicemen have been comforted by this book, and I am publishing it now in the hope that it may reach and benefit many people.

February 2014
With hands folded,
Kim Jae Woong

CONTENTS

The worldly events that unfold before you
are the realization of the way you have cultivated
your mind

1. Merit

Everyone wants to be happy and well-off, but one must first plant the right causes. When we constantly invoke a *won* (selfless vow or prayer) to plant merit[1] and put that prayer into practice, the vessel that contains our merit grows. Also, a frugal mindset that conserves material goods directly becomes merit. If you waste money, the god of money will leave you. The frugal mindset that values and conserves food, electricity, or anything of worth brings merit and blessed fortune. Good fortune is not something that you ask for—you should actively plant its causes, and how much you reap will depend on how much you have sowed.

---

[1] Merit (*punya* in Sanskrit, *bok* in Korean) is the store of wholesome karma created by the performance of virtuous deeds, which bear fruit in the form of happiness in the future.

One who has planted much merit will feel secure even during a recession, but one with little merit will shiver with anxiety as the economic crisis deepens.

Thinking that anything we take becomes ours is the mindset of a thief. Hoping to become rich at one stroke is also the way of a thief. Such a mindset tries to possess things out of greed, without paying due cost and effort.

A charitable mind that wants to help others brings merit. Our mindset towards Buddha should also be one of gratitude and reverent service, rather than one of begging and wanting things from him. Among us and around us, there are those suffering from serious illnesses, or who are in distress having declared bankruptcy. Compared to such people, how fortunate we are! Unaware of such blessings, if we keep wanting more, asking "Lord Buddha, please promote me at work,"

"Please make me earn more money," or "Please let my children get into a good school," then our affairs will not run smoothly. It is when we practice the mind of serving Buddha with reverence that the Bodhisattvas who serve Buddha think favorably of us and help us. The more you practice gratitude, the more merit you receive.

Our karmic ties with the orphans living in our neighborhood are profound indeed. They are not strangers, for they may have been our children in the past, or may become our children in the future. In our pursuit of finer clothes, nicer food, and bigger cars, we are always busy and in need of money. If we could save just a little and care for those children, the spiritual richness we feel when we help them is something that could never result from pursuing any of the Five Desires (Desire for wealth, sex, fame, food, and sleep).

The law of karmic causality is exact. When you accumulate merit, you receive good fortune, and when you accumulate bad karma, you receive the consequences of this bad karma. However, even if you have planted bad karma, it melts away when you plant merit. In the city of Daegu, there were three Christian women, in their late fifties and early sixties, whose children had all grown up. After having consulted with their families, they decided to volunteer for the less fortunate people for about twenty days each month. Each person took charge of fifteen to twenty households and cared for the elderly people who lived alone there. For about seven years, they worked ceaselessly, washing the clothes of the elderly residents, cleaning their homes, providing fuel, and preparing meals and *kimchi* for them. What fruitful and fragrant lives they led! An enlightened master who saw these women realized that the negative karma from their past lives had all been wiped out, owing to the merit of sincerely caring for others.

Before you start a business, you should realize the level of your merit. Money is earned by the power of merit, and not by the desire to earn it alone. Pursuing a goal with greed or recklessness should be avoided. You must first consider whether it can be achieved in the light of your health, ability, and time available. If you think it is not possible given these constraints, you should dedicate enough time and resources beforehand. Goals cannot be achieved by simply pushing ahead with your plan. If your mind is full of haste, you will invariably fail, due to the greed in the mind. In such situations, you must surrender[2] the hasty mind and read the Diamond Sutra to calm your mind, and invoke a fresh won before renewing your efforts. It is not the body but the mind that accomplishes things. Nothing turns out well with a hasty mind. Only

---

[2] Surrendering is a method of cultivating and purifying one's mind by offering up the thoughts, emotions, and delusions to Buddha by reciting *Mireukjon Yeoraebul*, the future Buddha's name. Instead of Buddha's name, you can recite the mantras or the name of deities and saints of your own belief.

when you realize the emptiness of greed and calm the mind, things can be achieved smoothly.

When you are running a store and business is lagging, instead of being troubled by the lack of customers, try to surrender that troubled feeling. As long as you are stuck with the troubled mind, the mental wave it creates will completely fill the store with an annoying energy. Even if a customer wanted to come in and shop, he or she would sense the negative wave, for human minds are that sensitive, and the customer would lose interest and not go in. Even if a customer did come in, the negative wave would make him or her leave quickly. Surrendering anxiety and disturbing thoughts is the actual practice of attracting customers. Also, thinking one's business is slow should be avoided. You should avoid even letting those words out of your mouth. When others ask you how business is, it is better for you to say that it is going well. Indeed, you yourself should actually have the mentality that your business is going well. In the end, it is the conditioning of a positive and successful mind that achieves goals.

The worldly events that unfold before you are the realization of the way you have cultivated your mind. When your attachments are strong, the world will become dark, but if you shed your attachments, the world will be simply radiant and blissful. This world is endowed with everything. It contains within it all that people seek. Yet, people do not attain what they seek because they impose upon themselves the mind of impossibility. If you are free from the negative, angry mind that insists "It is not possible," things become possible.

Just as enlightenment is attained through due preparation, everything in the world is achieved through preparatory wons and actions. No matter how difficult a task is, if you make thorough, adequate preparation, you can work with confidence, and will be able to accomplish it successfully.

When people look for a spouse, become friends with someone, or hire an employee, it always happens that people of a similar level of merit or wisdom find one another. As the saying goes, "Like calls to like." The type of parents a person is born to or the success of one's business all depend on how much merit one has planted. In the law of merit, there is never the slightest error. Since we meet people and live the life we live according to the amount of merit we have planted, how can we blame anyone else or complain about our lot? We must diligently invoke wons to plant great merit before Buddha, both for the present and for the future. If you invoke wons, you create the awareness that you should plant merit, and will also encounter opportunities to plant merit.

If you want to do something, or if you are having a difficult time achieving it, invoke a won: "May this goal be fulfilled brightly so that I can serve Buddha well, *barwon*[3]!" Although things that are beyond your level of merit cannot be achieved, if you keep planting merit and your merit reaches a sufficient level, your won will surely be realized. Buddha's Dharma is mysterious—even if your words are seemingly impossible, if you invoke a grand and radiant won before Buddha, it will eventually come to fruition.

A person cannot give his merit to others, nor can one take away others' merit. Just as in the saying, "The shadow of Suyang Mountain stretches eighty *li*," even if there is only one person in the family who has planted merit in the past, many people will benefit from the power of that merit. However, one cannot give merit to others. There can be no merit where none has been planted. Merit must be planted constantly. Also, when a misfortune strikes,

---

[3] In Korean, "I offer up this won to Buddha."

the vessel of one's merit can become cracked, so that the merit seeps out. Therefore, one must read the Diamond Sutra diligently every morning and evening and always practice surrendering without losing mindfulness, in order to preserve the accumulated merit.

An enlightened master once visited a certain family. Although the family members appeared to lack merit, the household was a prosperous one. Thinking this strange, he looked more closely at the family and noticed that their dog had planted great merit in its past life. In this case, the family was wealthy thanks to the blessed fortune of the dog.

An enlightened master once said that if you find water after suffering from thirst, you should throw away the remaining water after saying, "May another thirsty person drink this." Such a person will not receive the retribution of being thirsty again. However, the mindset of thoughtlessly throwing away the water after gladly quenching one's thirst will once again invite the karmic retribution of suffering from thirst.

Every time you receive a paycheck, try to look back and see whether you have worked with the mindset of earning three times your wages for the company. If you can do this, you are a wise person, for you receive the results of causes that you have planted. It is not that you must physically work three times as hard, but if you work with such a mindset, you will pay detailed attention to everything you do. Such an attitude will positively influence your surroundings, and help others plant merit along with yourself. The merit planted in this way belongs to you and not to others. Thus, there is no need to seek recognition for planting your own merit.

If your mindset is that of avoiding work and finding everything bothersome, this is the mind of a lazy person. If you do not cleanse that mind, you will have no place to stand confidently.

The mind of a wealthy person is a mind that regards all work as his own work. Whether it is another person's task or your own, whether it is pleasant or difficult to do, if your mindset is never to let the body be idle, and diligently look things that you can do, you will then become wealthy as a result of such a healthy mind.

If we endeavor to become more enlightened and full of merit together with the people around us, our mind's vessel becomes larger and broader to the same extent. Such a mindset is the mind of planting merit and the mind of an owner.

The speech of a person who has planted much merit is gentle, yet it has strength and dignity. This is the power of the merit accumulated in one's mind.

A sentient being's mind is attached to eating. A person's heart will soften when he or she is served a meal, for a meal represents not only food, but the caring mind of the host as well. At that moment, merit accumulates in the mind of the host. There is a saying that the merit of serving a meal to one good person is greater than the merit of serving meals to one thousand thieves, and the merit of serving a meal to one spiritual practitioner is greater than that of serving meals to one thousand good people. There is also a saying that you must accumulate merit before an enlightened master whenever there is a chance to do so. Regardless of what life or situation you are in, you will be the first to receive help. Enlightened masters gladly accept offerings that are made out of devotion and reverence, otherwise they are not likely to accept them.

We must give away the things that we do not need, and give to those who cannot repay us. If we give to people who can repay us, we develop a mindset that expects payment or benefits in return. We should generate the mindset of giving to purify our greed. While being generous to others, we must be strict with ourselves. By practicing the mind of giving unconditionally, we plant the causes to receive good things both in the present and the future.

People who manage household budgets are constrained by the anxiety of having to live within certain limits for the month. Many people live with this sense of deficiency, and how desperate their minds must be! If they imprint such a notion in their mind and do not cleanse it, they will become poor in this life and in their next life as well. Even if a person does not have material goods at this moment, if he has a "plentiful mind," he will have plenty of material goods in accordance with that mind.

Seemingly insignificant thoughts accumulate one by one to form the basis of our stability. We must surrender our mind of deficiency and practice the mind of plenty.

It is said that a single person cannot eat more than forty sacks of rice in his entire life. People, whether poor or rich, must eat three times a day. Thus, a wise person is content with an adequate level of wealth, and cultivates the mind and plants merit instead of pursuing endless greed. No matter how wealthy a person is, all he or she really needs from day to day is simple clothing, food, and a place to live. We use these items only briefly, and then we leave them all behind to Nature and depart from this life.

If we go to work and run our businesses for Buddha and to make Buddha's mind happy, our bodily discomfort will be relieved.

We plant merit in the mind. When we make an offering to Buddha, the merit is planted in the mind that perceives the act of offering. Protecting and spreading Buddha's Dharma (teachings), guiding others to read the Diamond Sutra, and establishing and caring for Buddha's monastery are all types of work that become merit. Merit is also planted in the moment when a person deeply invokes the sincere mind to plant merit before Buddha, and when deep reverence and bliss are awakened.

If you lend money to someone, lend with the intention of simply giving it to that person without the expectation of being repaid, and do not think about it afterwards. If you practice this, your mind will neither become attached to the money nor the person who borrowed the money. You will be undisturbed whether you are paid back or not. Also, when you give material objects to someone, do not give for that person's sake, but instead to make Buddha happy, and to cleanse yourself of the mind that dislikes giving—the mind of greed. Even if it begins with an empty gesture, if you diligently practice the mind of giving, your mind will become broader and your attachment to material goods will disappear, purifying the mind of greed.

If there is a person who plants merit without having the notion of "I" and whose purpose of planting merit is to make Buddha happy, that person will offer up the very notion that merit has been planted.

A person who cultivates the mind does not covet the merit he has planted. Like a toy tied to a string, the planted merit can be brought to the person at any time. If a person has the mentality of wanting to receive the benefit of that merit, the merit will decrease, but if he offers up the merit to Buddha, it will become even greater merit, and he will fully imprint Buddha in his mind. At that moment, the mind becomes enlightened, and the ego melts away.

Since the Dharmakaya ("truth body" or the true nature of Buddha) is present anywhere and everywhere, when you offer up something to Buddha, that place is the Dharma hall, and the place you awaken reverence is the Pure Land. When you lack or desire something, surrender all such minds to Buddha, and before using something, if you always offer it up to Buddha, you will plant the "Great Merit of No Limit" which gives you anything you need at the time you need it. It is said that when a Bodhisattva wishes to make an offering to Buddha, the offering simply appears on his outstretched palm. Through the virtuous merit of having made offerings to Buddha for countless lives, the Bodhisattva's wishes are immediately realized.

The Great Merit of No Limit means that you can obtain whatever you need whenever the need arises, even though you may not have such things in ordinary times. When you have something valuable, you have to worry about taking care of it and protecting it from being stolen. But with the Great Merit of No Limit fulfilling your needs whenever they arise, there is no reason to worry. If there is no notion of deficiency in a person's mind, his or her face also shines with merit. The Great Merit of No Limit is attained through eradicating all sense of deficiency, being liberated from neediness, and planting great merit before Buddha. Such a person's blessed fortune will never run out, no matter how much blessed fortune he or she receives. By practicing reverence and devotion to Buddha, delighting yourself in the realm of enlightenment, by offering up your mental and physical service to make Buddha happy, and by practicing the mind of helping others to enlighten their true nature, you plant the Great Merit of No Limit.

A household with a person who plants merit will be blissful, just as a country where many plant merit will be prosperous. A household with a person who cleanses karmic hindrances will be harmonious, just as a country where many cleanse karmic hindrances will grow stronger. Cultivating one's home and country to make them a brighter place is the duty of a spiritual seeker.

Just as merit is of vital importance in this world, it is also important in the world of cultivating the mind. Everything, whether becoming enlightened or entering a radiant realm, requires virtuous merit.

One day, Venerable Aniruddha, one of the ten great disciples of Sakyamuni Buddha, was trying to sew his clothes. Because of his blindness, however, he could not put the thread into the needle. So, he thought to himself, "If there is someone who wants to plant merit, may that person come and thread this needle." The person who came to help him was none other than the Buddha himself. Realizing who it was, Venerable Aniruddha asked the Buddha, "Lord Buddha, why do you wish to plant more merit, when you have planted so much already?" Lord Buddha replied, "Aniruddha, no one is more eager than I to plant merit. If sentient beings truly understood the root of all evil, and the consequences of their sinful thoughts, words, and actions, they would never fall into the three evil realms. But because they do not know this, they continue to fall. I must plant merit for their sake. Of all the powers in the world, the power of merit is the greatest. With the power of merit, one attains enlightenment."

2. The Body

The way a person uses the mind
continues to shape the face

When our attachment to the body is very strong, emotions have greater control over us. Only one who is liberated from attachment to the body is a truly free person. Therefore, we are free only inasmuch as we have cultivated and emptied the mind before Buddha.

When people become ill, they think it is just a problem with the body. They do not normally think that it could be caused by a certain mindset in their present life or karmic retribution and karmic hindrance from their past life. Going to a good doctor or taking good medicine is only a temporary solution in such cases. It is when we thoroughly surrender the cause that we can be fully cured of the illness.

When the body is sick, the mind becomes sick as well. Because the mind thinks that it is in pain, the bodily pain can sometimes become even worse. Even though the body is sick, the mind should remain healthy by surrendering to Buddha well.

Instead of hoping to avoid illness, when we are sick, we should surrender to Buddha the mind that arises in our sickened state. When healthy, we should surrender the mind that arises while in a healthy state.

Each time a person becomes angry or annoyed, the mind generates poison. This poison spreads to internal organs and the entire body, and in some severe cases, the face, the hands, and feet may become swollen. If the venomous mind does not settle down, the person will remain in the most hellish of hells, and anything he or she touches will be broken.

When the poison in the mind gushes out in the form of greed, it causes diseases in the digestive organs such as stomach cancer, ulcers, or gastritis. When it explodes in the form of anger, it causes problems in the lungs and respiratory organs. Sores on the head and the body are also caused by the spread of poison and hatred generated in the mind. Combined with fatigue, the mind's poison can also lead to fever and body aches.

When anger arises, misfortunes follow. On a physical level, as many as fifty thousand white blood cells are destroyed, the blood pressure rises, and one's vision becomes blurred. Anger should be surrendered absolutely.

When a person has reverence for Buddha, all the internal organs become healthy, thanks to the merit of having generated such a radiant mind.

A person whose soul and spirit remain within the body will be healthy in both body and mind. Because most people turn their attention to things outside the mind, following things such as money, work, or people they like or dislike, they live with an empty (absent-minded) body. Swayed by passions and emotions, likes and dislikes, their mind goes busily back and forth, in and out of the body. Surrender the mind that likes or dislikes someone by reciting Mireukjon Yeoraebul, Mireukjon Yeoraebul, Mireukjon Yeoraebul.[4] Then, you will feel serene.

Try surrendering even the mind that feels hot. Then, though the body may be a little bothered by the heat, the mind will not be. Whether one feels hotter or cooler depends upon a single notion. In any case, we need to be able to master the body.

---

[4] Mireukjon Yoraebul (Korean): Maitreya Tathagata. The name of the next Buddha.

If one's attachment to the body is extreme, the body may feel like a great heavy weight that one has barely enough strength to drag around. The attachment to the body clings tightly to comfort and likes only what is easy and convenient. As the attachment is cleansed, the body feels lighter because the mind has become healthier.

When you have to do something, do not cling to the notion that you must do that particular task. Rather, try surrendering that notion before doing the work. The mind will be much less burdened. Also, when you meet someone, surrender the feeling of like or dislike. Then, you will be less affected by the emotions that arise because of that person. Even when you are going to sleep, if you fall asleep while surrendering to Buddha the notion of being asleep, your surrendering will continue throughout the night. This helps greatly in cleansing the attachment to sleep.

It is only natural to rest when we are exhausted. We do not have to rest while clinging on to such notions as "I am not up to the task," or "I am worn out." It would be better to rest with a lightened mind after offering up these thoughts to Buddha. Whatever you do, it is the work and the body that are busy, and it does not help if the mind becomes busy too. If the practice of surrendering the busy mind continues, our actions will be swift while the mind remains at ease.

It is said that the shape of one's face comes from the shape of one's bones, and the shape of one's bones comes from the shape of the mind. For a person's face to change, his or her basic mindset must change. By the age of twenty-seven, even our brain cells have been completely replaced through the process of metabolism. A person therefore has a totally different body from the one with which he or she was born, and is thus completely independent of his or her parents. The way a person uses the mind continues to shape the face.

Practicing hatred or blame towards others even for a week makes our face look somewhat peculiar. At such times, applying expensive makeup will not make the face look any better. Rather, we should apply makeup to the mind—or in other words, practice surrendering the mind of hatred.

If one's mind is that of praising and respecting the good qualities of others, the face will appear very noble and virtuous. Also, if a person always practices a positive mentality, the face is bright and radiant.

If the mind is suppressed or restrained too much, it can bring negative side-effects to the mind or the body. A person who can reverently surrender the arising mind and discipline both the mind and the body is a truly able person.

When sexual desire arises, it is not right to shun or despise such thoughts. It is even less helpful to restrain or suppress them. We should surrender the thought to Buddha and realize the true nature of lust. From mishandling this emotion, there are many occasions when unfortunate consequences result.

If sexual desire arises strongly, lower your intake of food, as it may be the result of over-nutrition. Touching both your ears with your hands is another way to calm the body and mind when lustful thoughts occur. Those residing in a monastery can circle the Dharma Hall with folded hands while reciting Buddha's name. Other methods of alleviating the desire include running in the fields, using jump ropes, busily occupying the body with physical labor, or taking a cold bath. If you have much free time, having a hobby is good as well. By any means, this obstacle must be overcome and cleansed from the mind.

There is a study showing that when a person prays with reverence, the quantity of the hormone that generates sexual desire substantially decreases. In other words, sexual desire arises when a person is lazy and absentminded. Once it arises in the mind, the body responds to it. If the desire does not arise, the body does not react. In reverse, therefore, if you practice surrendering intensely to the part of the body that is aroused, that part of the body subsides as if nothing had happened. Afterwards, focus your surrendering on the mind. In this way, even sexual desire can eventually be overcome.

Buddha once said in a Dharma lecture concerning people of the opposite sex, that you should see older people as a mother or father, those who are slightly older as an older sister or brother, and younger ones as a younger sister or brother. If you practice this teaching, it will help in cleansing the sexual desire.

The true nature of the "I" (ego) is attachment to the body. Being changeful and restless, it always runs here and there looking to do something. If things don't work out the way it wants, it is quick to lose its temper and lament, whereas if its goal seems to be fulfilled, it leaps for joy. Like this, bodily attachment is ready to cling on to anything, but with the mind that offers up to Buddha, bodily attachment and karmic retributions melt away.

An essential requirement for attaining wisdom is to plant merit before Buddha with the body. Merit means that one has no regret or shame toward one's body. As a result of having planted merit, the world feels like a gentle place. In other words, it is the state where misfortunes are calmed. When we surrender every arising thought to Buddha and do everything with the mindset of making Buddha happy, the body will accumulate merit, and the mind will become gentle enough to attain peace and awaken to wisdom.

The right posture, the right attitude, the right way of walking, and the right words all come from the right mind. And the right mind, in turn, is formed by right actions. The practice of organizing our shoes neatly, hanging our clothes tidily, and keeping our belongings in an orderly manner all greatly influence how we organize our mind.

If my mind generates a bright mind, then due to the merit of having generated such a mind, the body that contains the mind will receive positive and calming energy. Generating a poisonous mind will cause others to treat me with a poisonous mind.

If I generate an arrogant mind, people will treat me with arrogance. Since the arrogant wave is transmitted to them, they treat me with an arrogant wave. Therefore, lower yourself humbly and practice reverence.

Rather than having the mindset of seeking something from Buddha, try to offer up everything to Buddha. Offer up your meal to Buddha before you eat, and offer up all your hungry, anxious, and painful minds as well. When practicing the mindset of giving, the giver's mind is happier and more confident than that of receiver. How much more so when one is giving to Buddha?

We must surrender to Buddha the mind that is busy serving the body. Knowing that we are always in death's shadow, we should candidly examine our lives. We should ask ourselves, "How am I living my life? What am I struggling for? What is my reason for living?"

Whatever you do, you should invoke a won first. Do not approach the task burdened by your preconceived notions or your desire to do the task.

Wisdom is not something acquired from certain formalities and procedures, nor does there exist a separate place for cultivating one's mind. Wisdom comes naturally when the mind connects with enlightenment, through cleansing the attachment to one's body and karmic hindrances.

It is better not to think about a person who has passed away. The energy of a dead person is like water and the energy of an alive person is like earth. If you think about a dead person often, your energy is taken away just as earth is washed away by water.

People who have killed many living creatures in their past lives are unhealthy and often fall sick. Also, while misfortunes such as being robbed or being involved in automobile accidents may appear to happen by chance, they are never mere coincidences. We must, therefore, avoid causing the death of a living creature, especially for our own specific need, by our request, or by our own act.

It is wise for a person who takes care of the elderly to provide them with enough spending money, so that they do not imprint in their minds the notion of "not having enough money." Furthermore, if they become ill, every effort should be made to help them recover from illness. If an elderly person goes on to the next life with the notion that the illness is not cured, he or she could suffer from the same illness again in the next life.

As long as a person has a body, his or her parents are deeply precious. The love of a parent for a child is just an extension of attachment to his or her body, and does not become much merit. However, the reverence of a child towards his or her parents goes against the attachment to the body, and thus becomes virtuous merit.

Buddha has said that of all beings that exist in the world, there is not a single being who has not been our mother or father in the course of *samsara*, the repeating cycle of birth and death. Since we form karmic ties ceaselessly and reincarnate endlessly, one who always shows compassion to his past and future parents and siblings is a wise person indeed.

Regardless of your gender or race, being born as a human being is a great blessing. For it is only when you receive a human body that planting merit and the practice of enlightening the mind can truly begin.

3. Human Relationships

I cannot cultivate someone else's mind
I can only cultivate my own mind

The uncultivated ego is sharp like a thorn. Because of loneliness, people cling to each other, but often hurt one another with the thorns of their ego. When those who have not cleansed the ego live together, there is more suffering than happiness.

When we are betrayed by a loved one, the shock of this experience sometimes leads us to harbor and cherish the humiliation, hatred, and pain throughout our entire lives. If we hold on to such notions, we cannot be mentally healthy. When we practice surrendering, however, the painful and unhealthy mind can be healed.

When you cannot control your mind, and become too close to someone, you practice the mind of expectation and demand certain things from the other person, all under the guise of affection.

Just as the darkest place is directly below the lamp, if you get too close to someone, that person's good qualities will not be visible, and if you stand too far away, neither good nor bad qualities can be seen. A practitioner should simply see others as Buddha.

Because all humans harbor the notion "I must survive," people are cold and indifferent to one another. They have been living while practicing this harsh mind of ego—putting me before my parents or siblings, and my own interest before that of my neighbors or my country—and they cannot be blamed for what is the innate nature of sentient beings. Just as Lord Buddha says in the Diamond Sutra, this is the way of the world and how we live our lives. Therefore, without losing one's mind to a person or to work, one should cultivate the mind by surrendering each mind as it arises.

Without the attachment to "I," the world would be peaceful and spacious. When "I" is involved, as in the case of such thoughts as "my father," "my people," "my wealth," and "my children," the world becomes narrow and uncomfortable. A person who cannot escape from the tangled net of "I" is a sentient being, and the concentrated notion of "I" is ego. One who cultivates the mind should see "I" and "others" as equal. Even when I need something, if another person needs it more, I should be able to give it away.

People are constantly frustrated that they cannot cultivate the mind of others. Like husbands and wives bickering, they criticize the ways of other people. However, if you look into your mind and offer up the causes of these disputes, which exist within the mind, all will become peaceful. Why always look outside the mind and try to find fault with others? I cannot cultivate someone else's mind. I can only cultivate my own mind.

Even if someone is angry at you, do not be angry in return. Even if you are struck with a blow, do not strike the other person in return. Even if you are being criticized, do not criticize others in return. Even if you are being mocked, do not mock the other. At that moment, look into your mind and see exactly who the focus of anger is, who is being beaten, who is being criticized, who is being mocked. Spiritual seekers should thus collect their minds and not be shaken any situation.

– The Heap of Jewels Sutra

Practice the mind of seeing the person you dislike as a reincarnation of Buddha, who has come to this world in order to enlighten your mind. Without this person, you would have missed a chance to purify the anger and hatred lying dormant in the mind. If you constantly practice the mind of seeing the person as Buddha, your mind will become broader, and the other person's mind will open up as well.

The act of hating someone arises because of the dormant hatred stored inside our mind. The hatred often acts upon somebody near us.

If the minds of dislike or hatred arise because of someone, rather than criticizing the person at that moment, trying to cleanse the hatred in one's mind is the way of a wise person.

If you find it entertaining to criticize other people, you should realize that there is anger in your mind.

Because an arrogant mind blocks out wisdom, it crushes the pride of others and incurs vengeance. Once a person incurs a vendetta in this way, he is bound to the chain of karmic causality, and will be caught up in the exchange of such vengeance for many lifetimes. When you pursue your spiritual practice with an understanding that you are lacking in many ways, you will gain wisdom and realize your own flaws.

Too much attachment to one's children can ruin their lives. A long time ago, there was a lady whose daughter planned to go to Germany as a nurse, but for various reasons her move was delayed. The mother had taken out a loan to finance her daughter's trip to Germany, so while her daughter was delayed for several months, she had to pay the interest on the loan, and her mind became anxious. When the mother asked Master Baek about this problem, Master Baek said that it was she who was preventing her daughter from going to Germany. Shocked by his answer, the lady asked what he meant by it. He said that every time her mind became anxious, wanting to send her daughter to Germany quickly, that mind engulfed the daughter and harmed her affairs. Such are the workings of the mind. Every time her impatient mind—thinking "My daughter must go," or "Why can't she go sooner?"—was transmitted to her daughter, the daughter's affairs fell into jeopardy. People do not know that their obsession or attachment to make their children prosper actually ruins their future. Therefore, when such thoughts arise, you must take notice and calm them immediately by surrendering. For the positive result that you desire for your children to be realized, you must invoke a won and plant merit for them.

If you can treat your children without the attachment that they are "my" children, you will gain wisdom, and can see clearly how they should live their lives. Also, when you offer them guidance in various ways with a serene and open mind, they will not rebel against you. However, if you restrain and nag at your children with a mind that holds on to "my" children, they will rebel against you and not listen to your words. When they sense your clinging mind, their minds are burdened and they suffer. Therefore, it is when we surrender such attachment that we can truly benefit our children.

Rather than thinking of your subordinates as people below you, have the mindset of learning from them. Without harboring the thought that you began your spiritual practice earlier than others, think that everyone is equal before Buddha instead. This way, you will not encounter situations where you become so embarrassed that your face blushes from shame.

People often say that it is better to respond to people's requests with a clear "Yes" or "No." Of course, there are affairs that need to be handled in such a way, but if you always respond carelessly, you may incur a loss or often hurt others' feelings. A person with a highly negative mindset will always say "No" from the start. A person with a positive mindset, however, will try to understand and accept the other person's mind first. If you accept his or her *mind* of request in a positive manner, the person will be content, regardless of whether or not the *request* is actually accepted. If the other person's mind is weak and unhealthy, and the request is denied outright, a feeling of vengeance will arise. Therefore, first accepting the other person's request by saying "Yes" and then saying, "Let's think how we could do this" will please the other person. If it turns out to be possible, it will be done. In the case that it is impossible, by explaining your current situation and asking the other person what they think the solution would be, no one's feelings will be hurt and matters will progress.

There is a saying that a kind word must be given in order for a kind word to return. More importantly, however, not just the words spoken, but the mind itself must be kind in order for kindness to be returned.

When you speak, do not speak to please the ears of others but to please their mind. Do not let your words become like arrows wounding other people's feelings.

When you express your sincerity, resonating from deep within the mind, with simple words, your humble expression can resonate within another person's mind and move him or her deeply. Therefore, rather than worrying about your lack of ability to express yourself, you must learn to safeguard the sincerity of your mind.

When a person is praised by others and becomes boastful or arrogant, it is a great setback in the cultivation of the mind.

As Buddha said, the person who points out our shortcomings is a noble teacher, for he shows us priceless treasures that are hidden from us. The Chinese Emperor Wu is said to have bowed three times with gratitude to anyone who pointed out his errors.

Everyone who enlightens me is my Buddha. Since every person has precious and enlightening qualities, if you learn and practice those qualities, it is as if you are meeting the Lord Buddha himself and putting his teachings into practice. There are Buddhas all around us. Buddhas at home, Buddhas at work, Buddhas in the streets, Buddhas on the bus . . .

We have to change the way we use our mind. One who can change a narrow and uncomfortable mind to a broad and peaceful mind is an able person. Because people cannot do this, they live in hellish agony, caught between feelings of inferiority and superiority, which arise at the slightest change of circumstances. Whether one feels inferior or superior, both thoughts are incorrect. Yet, people practice such a mindset repeatedly for many lifetimes until it hardens into a karmic hindrance. In the mind's pure original state, there is neither superiority nor inferiority. Nevertheless, as people live their lives and experience the exchange of thoughts and emotions, they become hurt and shocked in the process, and conclude with their dark reasoning that they are either superior or inferior. These two thoughts incur further karma, and because of the karma, they argue with one another, and in the end, they become entangled in the negative karmic ties. This is how sentient beings perpetuate the repeated cycle of life and death. In order to escape it, you should not become attached to the "I."

If there is something unusual about your state of mind as you interact with someone, it means that you have a karmic tie with him or her. In order to be liberated from the tie, you must cleanse that mind. When you feel longing or hatred for someone, promptly surrender that thought to Buddha. Even the tiniest fragment of emotion lying buried in your mind must be found and surrendered.

When the time comes to settle a debt with someone who has a negative karmic tie with you, you may suddenly develop a strong craving to eat meat. This could mean that you want to get revenge for the wrong committed against you in a past life. When people who have such murderous karmic ties meet in this life as spouses, siblings, friends, or colleagues, they naturally have very bad relationships. Therefore, you must not kill or harm a living animal. Especially, you must not point to an animal and say, "I want this chicken slaughtered," or "I want that fish caught." They could become obstacles to your eternal life.

A negative karmic tie with someone will not be resolved by simply avoiding the person or not thinking about him or her. Unless the notion of the karma itself is cleansed, it remains in our subconscious forever. Do not try to "cut away" the notion. If you try to sever it, it becomes even stronger. Even when surrendering to Buddha, if your intention is to forcibly eradicate the retributive karmic tie, it will hide from you. Therefore, while reverently offering up to Buddha all your notions about that person, treat them with kindness and be generous with material objects as well. This way, your negative karmic ties will melt away. Unless we are liberated from the ties of the retributive karma, we will be bound by them in all incarnations. However, no matter how strong and fateful the karmic ties may be, if you diligently practice surrendering in ordinary times, you can avoid them. And even if you encounter them, you will not get hurt so badly. Through the practice of surrendering, your mind will be wholly liberated in the end.

Even if you are visited by unwelcome guests, practice the mind of unconditionally serving them food and giving them money for their journey home. Because your mind is unwilling to give, even in dreams, such a practice is absolutely necessary in order to cleanse the mind.

One who has the mindset of serving Buddha well will have the same mindset of serving his or her fellow practitioners and taking care of other practitioners well. One whose mind is firmly grounded upon such a mentality is filled with the reverence of serving Buddha. When your mindset is one of helping others enlighten their minds, your mind naturally becomes enlightened first.

A deer in the forest wanders here and there in search of sustenance. Like this, a wise person walks alone, like a rhinoceros horn. Therefore, searching for the freedom of solitude, scorned by ignorant friends, go forth alone, like a rhinoceros horn! If you befriend a kind person, of wise and noble character, you can overcome all hardship. Therefore travel joyfully with that one, guarding your mindfulness. But if you cannot find such an one, then, like a king renouncing a realm he has conquered, go forth alone, like a rhinoceros horn! Like a lion undaunted by clamor, like the wind unsnared by the net, go forth alone, I say, like a rhinoceros horn!

– Sutta-Nipata

Buddha is the only place of warmth. Sentient beings treat each other coldly because their relationships are based on self-interest. When it is time to marry, they look for partners out of loneliness, but even when they find partners, the lonely mind remains. One's loneliness cannot be resolved unless it is cleansed from the mind. It is not just a problem for this life, but the next life and the life after that. In the outside world, people pacify the lonely mind by going out to drink and passing time with others amid noise and distraction. But when they wake up the next morning and return to their normal state of mind, the loneliness has not disappeared. Loneliness does not surface during times of busy activity, but when everyone has left, the loneliness remains behind, undiminished. It can be resolved only by cleansing the mind. Therefore, one must quickly find a way to develop a connection with Buddha, strong enough to last for all eternity.

If you meet and help others in order to serve Buddha, you imprint the radiance of Buddha in your mind, and not the darkness of those whom you help. If you remain attached to the notion that you have helped someone, the desire to be repaid may arise, and you will become attached to that person. Sometimes, you could even be born into that person's household in order to claim back what you gave to them. Furthermore, the ego's poisonous energy, which clings to the notion of having helped another, may bother that person, causing them to feel humiliated. But if you help and serve others with a mindset of making Buddha happy, there is no ego, and it does not generate any negative wave towards the other person.

When someone asks a question, answer him or her sincerely, and when you are not asked, do not force your teachings upon others.

You must practice the mind of lowering yourself, for the sake of your eternal life and for your present reality as well. If you practice the humble mind, your mind will be at ease and you will gain wisdom. As long as you do not put yourself above others, your relationship with others will be smooth.

When we treat others with a sincere mindset that reverently calls out "Lord Buddha," the mind will be at ease and respectful at that moment, and a radiant impression of Buddha is left in the mind. In the end, it is we who become more enlightened. If there is someone who sees everyone he or she meets as a Buddha, that person is probably also a Buddha in that instant.

A person who has someone to revere is a truly happy person. It is not the revered person who becomes happy, but it is we who become happy the moment that we generate reverence.

4. Social Interactions

The difference between a great person and
a lesser person lies in how much one has cleansed
the attachment to "I"

Only a person whose mind has no limitations can overcome his or her limits. Limitations are only self-imposed by the mind. In truth, the mind's ability is limitless. It is the same with the notion of not being able to do something. As you surrender the notion that you cannot do something, learn how to do it, and put effort into it, eventually you will gain the ability to do it.

Even if you were to live for just one day, or even for a single moment, you should live with the mindset of an owner. An owner's mind is the healthy mindset of caring for and tending to the place where you are, in order to make it a comfortable place for everyone to live.

There is a saying, "Work is love." If you do good work, everyone appreciates it. If you don't do what you should have done, everyone dislikes it.

The practice of surrendering while working will melt away attachment to the body. The lazy and selfish mind that avoids hard work and cares only about "my body" vanishes naturally. Therefore, reciting Buddha's name while working is a very good method of spiritual practice.

Too much stress can cause illness. When you keep surrendering the mind that feels stressed, the accumulated emotion dissipates, and the mind feels light and healthy. At the same time, the body that contains the mind will become healthy as well.

Even if he has the strength to carry the entire world, a wise person only handles what his hands can reach. If you have ten units of strength, you should take care to use only seven and keep the remaining three in reserve.

Try to live for just twelve hours a day. Trying to live twenty-four hours a day or even longer is a wearisome task.

Sometimes a feeling of burdensomeness arises because of a task you have to do. If you surrender that mind well, you will feel confident. This self-confidence comes from awakening an inner strength that will enable you to accomplish any task, no matter what it is, or when and where you have to do it. The truth is that an hour is still an hour, and a day is still a day's length, whether you have this burdensome feeling or not. When you surrender the mind that feels pressured to death, your mind will be composed and your actions will become swift. At such moments, your work and spiritual practice are not separate things.

Do not dwell on regrets. Try to commit fewer regrettable acts. If you happen to do something which your mind regrets, you should surrender the mind, and do many good deeds so that you do not have the regretful mind any longer.

A person was once passing by a field in autumn. Seeing how the millet crops were ripe and gold, he picked up a handful and ran his fingers through it, and the millet grains fell on the ground. In his next life, he was reborn in that household as a cow to repay the debt of the fallen millet grains. If you receive something for free and do not pay it back in this lifetime, you must repay the original amount several times over in your next life. If you owe a meal to someone, you must buy that person several meals in your next life. And if you strike someone with a blow, you will receive several blows in your next life. If that is the case, what will become of those who embezzle public funds or Buddha's wealth? They must pay back what they have taken for countless lives to come. Moreover, if someone passes on the stolen wealth to his or her children, wouldn't the children's future be bleak and hopeless as well?

The moment you think, "Because of that person" or "Because of so and so," you should be alert and surrender the thought immediately. It is when we realize that all things are consequences of the causes we have created, that we can become humble. A person who looks for the causes of wrongs in himself will advance and be successful, but a person who blames and condemns others has a long road ahead in his cultivation of the mind.

Because the three poisons of greed, anger, and arrogance exist in the mind, people torment each other with these poisons. But without realizing that the poison is within their own mind, people complain that the other person's poison is causing them to suffer, and place the blame on others. One who can lay the blame on himself is a person who has awakened to wisdom and gained spiritual maturity.

A person whose thoughts are full of loneliness is always lonely. A person who always thinks about lack of money spends his entire life with the mind of deficiency. A person whose thoughts are those of a beggar lives his entire life as beggar. A person whose mind is filled with arrogance can often experience failures, because he lacks the mindset of learning from a wiser person or from the world. Wisdom grows when we realize that all human preconceived notions are incorrect, and surrender those notions.

People experience difficulties and obstacles because of the difficulties and obstacles contained within their mind. Anything they do will therefore be full of difficulties. Others will treat them in ways that will cause difficulties as well. When our mind is positive and bright, when we humbly devote ourselves to resolve a task with sincerity, things will progress smoothly, and others will treat us with sincerity also.

If I generate an intention to deceive others, in response to that mental wave, others will try to deceive me as well. Therefore, do not generate the negative mind. If you handle your affairs with malice, you will suffer a loss before the other person does.

Practice the mindset of saying "Thank you," even if it does not come naturally. The uncultivated mind does not know how to be thankful.

Instead of thinking that others help them, people live with the thought that they are constantly sacrificing themselves for others. Because people are born with their own blessed fortune, regardless of which household they are born into, they live according to their own merit and not the merit of their parents. Indeed, there are parents who enjoy prosperity because of the merit of their children. Let us think "Everyone is helping me," and practice the mind of being grateful to the world that helps us.

Realizing the true nature of greed is like knowing the characteristics of water. If someone falls into water and flounders, he will sink even further by struggling to float. On the other hand, his body will stay afloat if he instead tries to go even deeper into the water. If you apply this principle wisely, it will help you when handling difficult situations in this world.

The way a person dresses shows his or her personality and spiritual progress. Choosing a color depends on one's taste, and one can see only to the extent of the mind's cultivation. Even if a better choice is offered, a person may reject it. One's way of dressing also reflects one's mental state. When the mind is disorderly, the colors of the clothes will likewise be jumbled. When the mind is tidy, one's outfit will be tidy as well. One's way of dressing and cultivating the mind are not separate.

Hoping that others will praise or recognize us is a sign that we are practicing a weak mindset. We must escape from being puppets swayed by other people's words. Whether a good or bad mind arises as a result of what the other person has said, surrendering it to Buddha, in order to restore calmness to our mind, is a wise thing to do and a way to nurture inner growth.

A boulder remains silent, whether it is rained or snowed upon, whether it is praised or blamed. For this reason, a boulder has dignity and virtue. If boulders could not hold back, but clashed together, wouldn't they break into mere pebbles? The qualities of the boulder would disappear, and all that remained would be pebbles that scrape noisily against one another. Therefore, stay calm and keep silent. Even when someone criticizes or slanders you, do not respond but restrain yourself, endure, and surrender. We should constantly practice the humble mind and lower ourselves.

Have you ever tried to swim across a river, and been worried that you might sink into the deep water while crossing it? Do not let your mind stay at the bottom of the water. Instead, let your mind be on the other side and swim across with your gaze fixed upon that spot. Never look towards the bottom of the river.

In dealing with worldly affairs, we should not have the mindset of attacking others, but we should also not lack the preparation to defend ourselves when others attack.

When you encounter a humiliating situation, you could have experienced such a mishap because of a subconscious recollection from your past life, or because of retributive karmic ties and hindrances. Therefore, when no one will listen to your explanation or appeal, surrendering your arising mind and calmly accepting the situation is a wise thing to do.

When a person generates a violent mind, the negative mental waves spread to the surroundings and disturb many people. On the other hand, the mind of reverence and joyful devotion emanating from a person can lead those nearby to a brighter path.

If you have no intention to learn from the world, your wisdom cannot grow and you will be separated from the wisdom of the universe. Your life will be one of complete darkness, both within and without. Practicing arrogance makes everyone dislike you, and attracts misfortunes. It brings no merit, and only ignorance. It presents darkness to the mind and suffering to the body. See everyone as Buddha. Then, you will discover the actions of all the future Buddhas, and will be able to learn from them.

If you are always lecturing others, you will practice the mind of learning from others less, and become boastful about yourself. Living this way, you direct your attention outside yourself and become good at scolding. However, it becomes harder to look inward and see yourself clearly. If we want to cultivate the mind and become enlightened, we must guard against such behavior.

If the individual members of a family try to practice the selfless and caring mindset toward one another, that family will prosper. Likewise, if there are many people who have the mindset of working with dedication for the sake of their company, that company will prosper as well. This is the way to become successful and cultivate happiness in the present life.

An arrogant person is hated and attacked by others wherever he goes. Because everyone thinks of themselves as superior, everyone dislikes an arrogant person. On the other hand, everyone likes a humble person. A humble mind gives out warmth to its surroundings.

How precious and fragrant is the humble and courteous smile, and the expression and the footstep of one who lowers himself? When you keep practicing the humble mind of lowering yourself, the wave from your warm mind spreads to the surroundings, and good things happen to you. Constantly practicing the humble mind of lowering oneself—this is cultivation of the mind.

Simply because you are earning a living, it does not mean that you are living a normal life. If a person's spirit decays through not having cultivated his mind, he cannot lead a healthy life. Only a person with wholesome spirit can lead an enlightening life.

The goal of spiritual practice is for the mind to become healthy. After your mind is awakened and you help others, you feel confident, but if you help others while you are still weak, you expect to be rewarded for your effort, and your mind gets lost in the act of helping

—hence you become even weaker than before. From a healthy self, there comes a healthy family and a healthy society.

The less ego a person has, and the more the mind is devoted to Buddha, the more benefit that person will bring to the household, society, and country. This is the type of person every country wishes for, and the whole world needs.

Wise people speak of ideals whenever they open their mouths. They speak of a better society, a radiant world, and about the realm of Dharma where people enlighten their minds. Ordinary people talk about events, and lesser people talk about the faults of others.

Regardless of your occupation, your primary goal should be to cleanse attachment to the body, which gives rise to the three poisonous minds—greed, anger, and arrogance. Then you will awaken bright wisdom and become free from the worries and cares of worldly life.

In the realm of the mind, there is no distinction between "I" and others, and all is connected as one. For this reason, in the scriptures it is written that when the mind of one person is pure, the minds of many are pure, and when the minds of many are pure, infinite beings are pure.

As long as there is at least one source of clean water flowing in to a well, it will never go bad, no matter how polluted it is. The person who cultivates his mind is like the source of clean spring water. It is for this reason that, since the old times, those who cultivate the mind are said to be the treasures of the nation.

A person who practices the Dharma should not only cultivate the mind well, but also practice compassion constantly, invoke wons, and pray before Buddha to ease the pain and sufferings of others.

The difference between a great person and a lesser person lies in how much one has cleansed the attachment to "I." A great person puts the public interest before his or her own interest.

Living for yourself, according to your own views, is the way to block out wisdom. The wandering thoughts in your mind are of no benefit to you, so offer them up to Buddha with utmost reverence. While practicing the mind of surrendering, if you can live to serve others and Lord Buddha well, your fragrant mind will fill the universe completely and make Buddha happy.

Hardship presents a perfect opportunity to cultivate the mind. When anger arises, recite Buddha's name to that mind until it calms down. If you keep practicing this, the root of the angry mind is cleansed, and you feel refreshed. Eventually, you will perceive the radiant realm of Buddha and your wisdom eye will open. After the root of the angry mind is completely surrendered, the realm of wisdom is opened before you. Then your mind is bright and cheerful, and is led to profound reverence.

A single mind determines not only the future of a person's life but also the future of a person's household. Combined with others, it determines the future of the country where such persons live together. If the people of a country practice a law-abiding and honest mindset and live frugally, this becomes the basis of great merit, on which the country will flourish. The minds of a country's people come together to decide the rise and fall of that country. When the minds of people change, the fortune of a household, society, and country all change as well. The mind is at the heart of all things.

5. Why We Should Cultivate the Mind

When I surrender this arising karmic hindrance,
I and the other both feel refreshed

We spend our days as if we will live forever. Death is something in the distant future, something that happens only to other people. However, as the Tibetan saying goes, who knows what will come first—tomorrow or the next life?

People live in the hope that tomorrow and the day after tomorrow will be a little better than today. However, if you do not cultivate the mind and plant merit in this present, the future will be no better in the least.

Buddha said that there is a treasure of infinite worth in our body, and this treasure is the mind. Just as this statement implies, the mind brings happiness or unhappiness depending on how it is used. We should surrender the negative attitudes that we have practiced for many lifetimes, and practice the positive mindset everyday so that our lives change for the better.

When I generate a certain mind, its mental waves spread out to the surroundings and echo back to me. A bright and healthy mind, a reverent mind, and a positive and caring mind—when the waves created by such a noble mindset return and touch myself and my family, this is called merit and blessed fortune. On the other hand, the mind-waves that spread and return each time I generate dark minds are called disaster and misfortune.

If we observe the minds that people generally practice in their lives, most live practicing the arrogant mind, boastful mind, resentful mind, criticizing mind, belittling mind, malicious mind, depressed mind, frustrated mind, pleasure-seeking mind, disheartened mind, and so on. Most people never realize that this is not the practice of bright, positive mind.

Because our mind has limitless potential, once it becomes replete with wisdom and merit through the practice of a bright mindset, it can even reach the level of Buddha. But people often bring misfortune upon themselves by misusing their mind.

Practicing your good points and correcting your flaws is the way of spiritual practice.

If life is stage play, you may as well play the part of a wise person.

If you imprint someone else's misfortune in the mind, it could become the cause of your own misfortune as well. Having imprinted it in your mind, if you are not able to surrender it, it could become your reality either in this or the next life. Some of the causes of misfortune are created in this life and others in our past lives. But even if we have planted many dark causes in our past, if we keep surrendering them to Buddha, the burden of misfortunes we carry will become lighter and lighter. Surrendering means intensively reciting Buddha's name on that thought, thereby making an offering of your mind to Buddha.

The practice of surrendering helps us to remove the dark-tinted glasses of our mind. People wearing dark-tinted glasses say that the world is dark even on a bright sunny day. When we surrender to Buddha the karmic hindrances that shroud our mind, we will finally come to realize that the world is bright and radiant.

A person who lives only for himself will develop an even stronger attachment to the body. It is when we generate the mindset of living for Buddha and enlightened teachers that the bodily attachment melts away. One who has left behind bodily attachment and the "I" will be a worthy human being and a Bodhisattva. Cultivating the mind is something that we must do in order to live like human beings. It is not an option that we can neglect. So long as you walk along a well-paved path, life is not painful and you can travel along it with ease. Yet, everyone rejects this path and walks through a trackless and thorny wasteland, lamenting dolefully that there is no path to follow.

The notions imprinted in your mind, whatever they may be, determine your present and future. Cultivating the mind means cleansing the dark notions within yourself; it is the process of offering up these notions to Buddha and enlightening the mind to return to its original pure state.

Even though a person may enjoy much wealth or a high position in society, without cultivating the mind, he or she cannot escape the realm of sentient beings.

Spreading the Dharma does not only mean recommending that other people should believe in Buddhism. By diligently practicing the Dharma, if you bring peace and order to the surroundings with radiant energy, lead others to have a good impression of Buddhism and its practitioners thanks to your virtuous deeds, and display through your life the benefits of practicing the Dharma, this is a great way of spreading the Dharma, without words.

While a person may not be a Buddhist, if his or her mind is thoroughly healthy and bright, such a person can be called a true Buddhist—since we follow the Dharma for our mind to become healthy and bright.

Whatever an enemy might do, whatever a murderous foe may do, there is nothing worse than the harm your own false mind can do to you. Whatever a father, mother, or relatives may do to help you, there is nothing greater than the happiness your own truthful mind can bring to you.

– Dhammapada (Verses of Dharma)

Because people do not know that greed, anger, and arrogance are the enemies that ruin their true self and eternal lives, they practice these minds even more. Once they realize this, it becomes much easier to cultivate the mind. Therefore, practice the mind of lowering yourself again and again, and try to see others as Buddha, over and over.

An uncultivated mind is poison itself. Therefore, how could we not cultivate the mind? When I surrender this arising karmic hindrance, I and the other both feel refreshed.

Upon reaching the level of Mahasattva[5], one can calm the minds of others. Since the power of a cultivated mind stabilizes the surroundings, this is a way of benefitting others.

Faced with a person with much greed and strong ego, people feel nervous and uncomfortable because of the negative spiritual energy from the person's uncultivated mind. The negative wave provokes the ego and poisonous mind of others, and they respond with negative minds and actions. On the contrary, faced with a person with little ego, people feel peaceful and delighted due to the positive spiritual energy from the person's purified mind. When a practitioner cultivates his or her mind to such an extent that no greed, anger, and arrogance remain, the bright energy from the purified mind calms the ego and the poisonous mind in others as well. Consequently,

---

[5] A great Bodhisattva who has practiced compassion for eons and reached a highly advanced level of enlightenment.

people spontaneously generate the mind of offering up something and paying respect to the practitioner of such a noble mind. We should empty our mind thoroughly to the point where others want to offer up something, and eradicate the ego thoroughly to the point where others want to bow down to us.

Things we should be grateful for are everywhere. How precious is the grace of the Heavens, and of Nature that surrounds us! Most people live unaware of this grace. Nor do they have gratitude to their parents, or for the effort of the many people who made it possible for us to have good food and clothes to wear. No wonder they do not have gratitude for Buddha, and in many cases, all they have is selfish greed and ego. Is this not the reality of sentient beings—to live each day in tumult with dark ignorance, incurring more and more negative karma? Perhaps that is why sentient beings have such a sad existence. We should diligently practice the mindset of gratitude.

How can we say that we own something simply because we paid for it? If we trace its history, even a bowl of rice is filled with the hard work and effort of all humanity. Therefore, we must offer it up to Buddha, who is the light of humanity and Nature, and eat with gratitude for the efforts of the people who have farmed, transported, and prepared it for us. Before meals, we should always offer prayers to serve Buddha well. Not only with food, but also with any other goods, the practice of gratefully offering them up to Buddha before receiving and using them is the way to live in accordance with the Dharma.

If you often practice the arrogant mind, your wisdom becomes dark. Without wisdom, you could easily encounter misfortune. In fact, even a beggar or a foolish person has an arrogant mind. Thoughts such as "If only I had been born into a wealthy family, I would not be living like this." are based on arrogance. In the path of spiritual practice, just as in other fields, you have to learn from those wiser than you in matters that are beyond your wisdom. Compared to other karmic hindrances such as greed or anger, arrogance is less noticeable, and is more difficult to cleanse. Thus it is said that your practice will progress only when you realize that your karmic hindrances are as massive as the earth itself. Also, you should regard others' faults and karmic hindrances as your own, and see others as Buddha. This way, even the deep-rooted arrogance can be cleansed.

All your wealth, fame, your spouse and children cannot be yours forever, and the mind that tries to possess them is the cause of all suffering and agony. Therefore, you must offer up to Buddha all worldly things, and must attain the wisdom and the Truth of Buddha, for these are not transient and can truly be yours forever. A state of having completely offered up the mind and body to Buddha, a wholly emptied mind, is the state of enlightenment.

If you keep looking back to the past, you are practicing a dead mind. There are also those who live only dreaming of the future. Such mind is barren indeed. A truthful life means being true to the present and surrendering the discriminative notions that arise at each moment. If you are true to the present like this, your past and future will naturally become truthful and enlightening. A truthful mind is the moment when Buddha's mind dwells within us. When Buddha is enshrined in your mind, your words and actions are reverent and courteous, and your spirit is awake.

We plant merit and commit sins with our mind. Even our experiences are ultimately the product of our mind. This one mind is like an artist. It can draw anything, and whatever it draws becomes reality. If you surrender your experiences and thoughts at the moment they occur without imprinting them, your mind will not be tainted.

See other people as Buddha. Spiritual seekers should enlighten their minds by seeing other people as the Buddhas of present and not as Buddhas of the future. How could you be surly and sullen before Buddha? Before Buddha, how could you not be humble?

If a person who treaded the spiritual path in the past lives do not cultivate the mind in this life, the lotus flower in his or her soul withers. When one learns the Dharma and cultivates the mind, the lotus flower blooms splendidly, emitting the fragrance of virtue and enlightening energy to the surroundings.

Depending on the mindset you have toward a certain task—whether you do it to please the Buddha's mind or for your own profit and fame—the results of the work will differ enormously.

No one can see their own eyes. This means that they do not truly know themselves. People cling on to their thoughts and view the world through them only. However, "my" thoughts are not correct. Even if correct, they are only correct at my own level. When the wisdom of my own level is surrendered, so that the mind is left like a blank sheet of paper, a brighter and more profound wisdom is revealed.

If your face's shape and expression are the result of how you have used your mind, you must awaken a determination to change them for the better by surrendering your erroneous mind and practicing reverence. People who do not know how to surrender continue their lives as they have always done, but those who cultivate their mind change their flawed mindsets, facial expressions, words, and actions by practicing the mind of living for Buddha. This is why they are precious.

We must diligently plant merit for a bright cause. We should work to realize the Heaven's will and Buddha's wishes by enlightening our mind and benefiting all humankind. If you do virtuous deeds with such a noble mindset, then in your future lives, when you awaken faith and resolve to tread the spiritual path, your circumstances will help you.

At the moment of death, if you generate reverence towards Buddha and recite Buddha's name, your spirit will become bright. If you practice surrendering in ordinary times, you will be able to surrender in times of urgency as well. People who cultivate the mind pursue spiritual practice all their lives in order to be able to recite Buddha's name at the final moment of death. Also, for the sake of the present and the next life, they perform good deeds and meritorious acts every day of their lives.

When the time comes, this body will die and decay, but the mind that dwells within the body will not die. According to the causes it has planted, the mind receives an appropriate body and starts a new life. Those who do not cultivate the mind are mostly reborn as animals. This is because to the uncultivated, hazy mind, everything looks like a human being. If you cultivate the mind brightly by surrendering well without losing mindfulness, and if you plant merit diligently, not only will you receive a human body, but you will be born in a more radiant place.

Heaven and the Pure Land are not far away. The devout mind that reverently serves God or Buddha, the serene and peaceful mind where the storms of strife and suffering have calmed—such a state of mind is the Heaven and Pure Land in that moment.

The craving mind is the source of all suffering. We should thoroughly surrender the craving mind, and transform it into a charitable and compassionate mind.

Wandering thoughts will only lead us to a hellish state of mind; surrendering will lead us to bliss and wisdom.

The mind is your eternal wealth and future. Cleansing the karmic hindrances buried in the mind, which are the source of your misfortunes, is indeed a worthy task.

6. How to Cultivate the Mind

To cultivate the mind means to empty it

However long you may have devoted yourself to Buddhism, if you do not know how to cultivate the mind, you will always remain on the threshold and never pass over it. Even though you can discourse at length about the philosophy of the Flower Garland Sutra or Lotus Sutra, if you do not know how to calm the suffering in your mind at this instant, what use is such knowledge in solving the problems of your reality? What is the use of knowledge if you cannot actually cleanse the dark thoughts emerging from the depths of your mind?

We should always practice looking into the mind. Only then can we surrender the arising mind without being deceived by it. If your mind is diverted towards the person you hate, making money, or fulfilling sexual desire, there is no time to look into your mind. If a karmic hindrance arises at such a time, it will be uncontrollable.

Constantly watching the mind is the basis of cultivating the mind. When the mind is always with the reverence of surrendering, one cannot be absentminded.

When the mind's gate is unlocked, temptation and misfortune force their way in and spread their roots. If a tiny pinhole is created, a karmic hindrance the size of a bull breaks in. A split second's absentmindedness can bring eternal regret. One should always remain on guard.

The only wealth that a sentient being has in the mind is greed, anger, and arrogance. A good way to cleanse the greedy mind is to practice the mind of giving constantly. When you cannot give material goods, practice the mind of giving without seeking rewards—even if it is just with your mind—and this will lessen your greed and broaden your mind's capacity. Anger is a great misfortune. To surrender anger is to surrender the misfortunes in our mind. Because anger is a terrifying fire that can burn away all one's accumulated merit in an instant, it is unwise to neglect it no matter how small it may seem. The arrogance that makes one think of oneself as great and better than everyone else is a dark and ignorant mind. It blocks out radiant wisdom. Therefore, you should treat everyone with a mindset that reverently calls out "Lord Buddha," always generate the mind of learning from the qualities of others, and forgive others' faults while never forgiving your own. One who has offered up all the wealth of anger, greed, and arrogance in the mind is an enlightened person.

Greed is the mind that craves for things beyond one's needs. It is a tenacious mind, like the mind of a wild beast.

Within greed, there is both greed for material goods (*kantamsim*) and greed for another person, which tries to possess another being (*umtamsim*). Greed is an unhealthy mind and a cause of poverty. Therefore, you must realize your actual needs, constantly practice the mindset of giving without expecting reward, and intensely surrender the greedy mind to Buddha in order to be freed from it.

Just as fire leaves only ashes in its wake, destruction is all that remains in the path of burning anger. Anger brings nothing but misfortune and lack of merit. It fills the mind with vengeance, and brings fiery karmic retribution to the body. Like fire, anger dries our blood and burns our flesh. Surrendering anger, however, brings virtuous merit.

When a person throws a stone at a dog, the dog chases after the stone. When a stone is thrown at a lion, however, the lion attacks the person who threw the stone. This is the wisdom of the lion. Likewise, when a wise person becomes angry because of another person, he does not quarrel with that person, but cultivates his own mind first.

Look into your own mind and cultivate your mind. These are the earnest words of Buddha.

The reason you do not like hearing the arrogant words of others is because you have arrogance in your mind. If you cleanse that arrogant mind, no matter how arrogantly the other person behaves, your mind will not react, but remain calm.

When your mind is uncomfortable, you should realize that your karmic hindrance has surfaced, and practice surrendering again and again.

The Diamond Sutra is the teaching in which Sakyamuni Buddha perfectly revealed his whole mind and way of practice. This Dharma lecture was given by Sakyamuni Buddha when his body and mind were at their healthiest. To use an analogy, his enlightenment was shining brilliantly like the sun at noon. Therefore, the Diamond Sutra is said to be radiance itself. When you reverently accept the Diamond Sutra—which embodies the entire mind and full radiance of Buddha—with your mind and body and read it, your mind is directed to Sakyamuni Buddha's bright mind from 3,000 years ago, and becomes one with that radiance. Thereby, the dark shades within the mind are liberated, eradicating misfortunes and enlightening your nature.

When we trust in the teachings of the Diamond Sutra and put those teachings into practice, karmic hindrances that are as big as mountains melt away. Knowing that all causes are within one's mind, surrendering every one of these causes to Buddha is the act of directly practicing the teaching of the Diamond Sutra.

When you are worried about something or encounter a difficult problem, reading the Diamond Sutra on the problem will gradually calm your mind, and in the moment when wandering thoughts subside, an enlightening answer can be revealed.

When you are reading the Diamond Sutra, there is no need to worry about being unable to concentrate or too many thoughts coming to mind. Such thoughts are what you have imprinted in the mind in your daily life, which are now emerging thanks to the radiant energy of the Diamond Sutra. If they continue to lie dormant within your mind, they will eventually become the causes of suffering. Since they are being driven out by the radiant energy, you will become comfortable.

There will be times when you feel tired of reading the Sutra. At such times, especially, you should plant merit. In spiritual practice, merit is like the oil that helps your practice progress smoothly. Try to plant merit before Buddha with material goods or, if you lack these, plant merit with your body, and also with your mind.

Reading the Diamond Sutra eradicates misfortunes. Normally, reading the Diamond Sutra in the morning frees us from misfortunes during the day, and reading before going to bed frees us from misfortunes during sleep. The human body is infested with dark organisms that constantly aggravate the body's owner. When we read the Diamond Sutra and cultivate the mind, such organisms find it impossible to survive, exit the body along with dead cells through the natural metabolic process, and are replaced by healthy cells. Because the Diamond Sutra is radiance itself, it does not allow darkness to remain. Medically speaking, a person's skin cells are replaced every 1,000 days, bone cells every 3,000 days, and brain cells every 9,000 days. If you read the Diamond Sutra throughout this time, as the dark organisms leave the body and are replaced with healthy cells, you become more and more radiant, and cannot encounter misfortune.

Not everyone who reads the Diamond Sutra will be prosperous and free from misfortune. We must avoid sin altogether, put great effort into cleansing the karmic hindrances we have accumulated over many past lives, and try our utmost to accumulate merit, in any way that we can. Only then can we be prosperous and free from misfortunes. If you do not cultivate the mind and accumulate merit, you waste your life and there is no hope of a bright future.

In the Diamond Sutra, it is often said that the virtuous merit of one who reverently receives the Sutra, reads it, and gives it to others is incalculable. However, even if you convey the enlightening words of Buddha to others, you must surrender the thought that you are performing this act. Such a thought is of no use to you.

You should give the Sutras only to those who will definitely read them. If the person who has received the Sutra mistreats it or steps on or over it, then due to the karmic retribution, he will be stepped on by others. When this happens, the person will try to get his revenge on the person who gave the Sutra. Therefore, how could we not be careful? In the Sutra of Karmic Causality, there is a passage that tells the story of a person who threw a Sutra on the ground, and became a hunchback in his next life as karmic retribution. According to Buddha's Dharma lecture, if you enshrine the Diamond Sutra and read it well, Buddha will surely see this, and the radiant energy of the surroundings will protect the place where the Sutra is kept.

Let a wise man blast away the impurities of the self, just as a smith blasts the impurities of silver, one by one, little by little, and gradually over time.

– Dhammapada (Verses of Dharma)

Cultivation of the mind is not something that you should try to achieve quickly over a short period of time. If you do not finish it in this lifetime, you continue in the next life and for countless lives to come. If you have difficulty reading the Diamond Sutra, rather than forcing yourself to read it, offer up a prayer, "May all sentient beings read the Diamond Sutra well to serve Buddha well, barwon." Naturally, you will find yourself reading the Sutra again.

Putting excessive effort into the practice is the mind of greed. Complaining that your practice is not progressing is the mind of anger. Thinking that you have made much progress is the mind of arrogance. To an enlightened person, there is no discrimination between reading the Sutra five times or seven times a day, or having practiced for five years or ten years. Instead of setting a goal that is too difficult to achieve and eventually giving up, read the Sutra with reverence whenever you are able to, and surrender the mind every time a thought arises by reciting Buddha's name throughout the day.

When you cultivate the mind, you regress to the past and cleanse the mind. When you cultivate the mind today, you liberate yesterday's mind. When you cultivate the mind on the following day, the mind of three and four days ago becomes liberated. By continuing to regress to the past like this, negative minds will be resolved.

Between three and five in the morning, the energy is bright and pure. This is the time when Bodhisattva Manjushri gives his Dharma lecture. By practicing at this time, you receive the life energy of the universe in full. They say that people who are active late at night often run into misfortunes. A way of living in accordance with the energy of the universe is being active when the energy is bright and sleeping when the energy is dark. This way, your mind and body will become healthy. You must also continue the practice until you go to sleep, so that your practice will continue throughout the night until the moment you wake up. If you fall asleep while being absentminded, you remain absentminded throughout your sleep, and your mind will not be clear even after you wake up. Since taking a nap is also practicing a dark mind during the bright day, it is better not to take naps if possible.

Reading the Diamond Sutra in the morning and at night, and reciting Buddha's name to the arising thoughts and situations that you encounter every day are the act of taking out everything that has been stored in the mind and offering them up to Buddha. There is no greater offering that we can make to Buddha.

People usually say that the most important phrase in the Diamond Sutra is, "One should exert the mind without attachment." However, this effectively describes a state of complete enlightenment. In our case, when we are still cultivating the mind, how can we hope to "exert the mind without attachment" when the mind is brimming with 84,000 karmic hindrances? If we are not swayed by the arising thoughts and emotions, and continuously surrender each one to Buddha, we will eventually be able to "exert the mind without attachment."

All my thoughts are incorrect. Even if they are correct, they are only correct at my own level. When the thoughts at my level have been surrendered and the mind is left empty, a wisdom that is greater and more radiant than "I" will be revealed.

In order to straighten the crooked mind, deepen the shallow mind, broaden the narrow mind, soften the sharp-edged mind, and transform a dark mind into a bright one, we first need the wisdom to realize our own shortcomings. If we acknowledge that our preconceived notions are incorrect and surrender them, our wisdom will grow immensely.

Do not let your mind dwell on unpleasant thoughts, and do not try to suppress them or distract yourself with other tasks. Instead, simply recite Mireukjon Yeoraebul to the unpleasant thoughts with reverence. If you do this, after some time, you will feel at ease in the end. This practice is how one "surrenders" (or conquers) the mind as Buddha says in the Diamond Sutra.

The mind is inherently empty and tranquil, but through the practice of anger, greed, and arrogance, this pure mind has become tainted. Surrender this tainted mind to the radiance of Buddha. There is no karmic hindrance that cannot be surrendered before the radiance of Buddha.

For one minute, practice surrendering with reverence before Sakyamuni Buddha, offering up all the bad memories, worries, frustration, resentment, and conflicts that weigh down your mind.

Buddha Dharma is the act of purifying the discriminative notions, wandering thoughts, and delusions that arise at each moment. It is problematic to pursue the Dharma while living an everyday life that is not in accordance with it.

Enlightened masters of the past taught people to sever the

mind of greed and suppress the mind of anger. However, in our complicated modern age, the way to cultivate the mind is to become aware of the greedy mind and surrender the angry mind. Realizing the greedy mind means that—since we cannot wholly do without the material goods to sustain our bodies—we should realize our true material needs and not seek more. Suppressing the mind of anger is like compressing a spring. It may explode even more violently, or cause stomach or heart disease. Therefore, the mind of anger should be surrendered to the deity or saint of a person's faith. Arrogance is the belief that you are better than everyone else. As this mind cannot be seen easily, we should practice the mind of humility, see others as Buddha, and always have an attitude of learning from others.

Holding on to wandering thoughts is a dark practice, but if you surrender them to Buddha, your mind feels light and refreshed. As you do the dishes, clean the house, or go for a walk, if you constantly practice surrendering each and every arising thought by reciting Mireukjon Yeoraebul to it, your mind will always be one with the Buddha and remain in a radiantly awakened state.

When you are talking with or listening to someone, practice surrendering diligently. Even if the other person speaks with an angry mind, if you surrender while you listen, the other person will also become calm. If you practice surrendering while you speak, you can control your emotions and you will benefit from brighter wisdom. With the mindset of surrendering at every moment, even between breaths, we should diligently offer up our thoughts.

When someone criticizes or insults you, if you perpetually harbor the notion that you have been insulted, like an inscription engraved upon a rock, it will be very painful for you indeed. Life will be much easier if a notion engraved on the mind can be forgotten just after a few days, in the same way that writing on sand is soon erased when the wind blows. Even better is to calm the emotion or thought on the spot, by surrendering it at the very moment it arises—just as writing on water disappears without a trace.

Since all disturbing thoughts only come from my mind, we must immediately surrender them to Buddha. We must surrender even the notion that we are surrendering and all the remnants of such thoughts as well.

Since there is no end to the number of discriminative notions in the mind, we must continuously surrender, and if no thoughts arise, we should surrender the notion that no thought is arising.

In the case of those who read the Diamond Sutra and cultivate the mind, what should they do when someone slanders their teacher? They should look into the mind and surrender their emotions by reciting Buddha's name to that mind. All the images and events in the world are simply shadows cast by one's mind. Therefore, always look into your mind, search within your mind, and never seek outside of it.

Surrendering does not mean suppressing or restraining one's thoughts and emotions, but directly and unconditionally reciting Buddha's name to the arising mind. By surrendering the mind, we can cure our inner problems and uproot the wrongful habits that cause us to commit sins. This means not only offering up the negative causes that lie hidden in the depths of the mind, but also offering up every habitual and emotional discriminative notion, without allowing even a speck of it to remain.

Absentmindedness means that we are being lazy in keeping watch over our mind. Since we never know when basic karmic hindrances such as laziness, malice, or lust may suddenly arise from our inner world, we should be as wary as someone walking on thin ice, and never be absentminded.

Bowing down to Buddha in the Dharma hall or making offerings to Buddha with material goods is the practice of surrendering the mind through such offerings and actions. Sometimes, however, as we bow down to Buddha, we let the mind attach itself to the statue of Buddha, which has no mind. We must be aware that the Buddha statue represents the Dharmakaya, who exists as Truth itself, without any shape or form, and pay our utmost respect while bowing down to the mind that reverently calls out "Lord Buddha."

Very often we picture Buddha or Jesus based on our own thoughts, and turn them into our idols. Those thoughts are our own, and exist only at our level.

Do not think of Buddha as an icon or personal image, but simply practice the Dharma with the mindset that reverently calls out "Lord Buddha," and the mindset of being present before Buddha.

When you practice surrendering, it is good to recite in the *janggwe* position, with both knees on the floor and keeping the hips and back straight. Usually, practitioners recite in units of one hour, because our karmic hindrances arise and subside in hourly cycles. The period in which a karmic hindrance rises and falls can be as short as one hour, or as long as three days, seven days, one hundred days, three years, nine years, or lengths of time beyond our comprehension.

People who walk towards enlightenment one step at a time, in order to remain true to their inner world, must not be disturbed by affairs of the outside world. When these outside events cease to disturb them, the karmic hindrances, lying deep within the inner realm, become more clearly visible. A person whose practice has matured and whose ego has melted away is as tranquil as an empty sky.

If we can offer up to Buddha all our thoughts, both good and bad, our mind will always be positive and bright. In other words, we are transforming our mind into Buddha's mind. It is not material objects of great value that Buddha wishes to receive from us, but the minds of hellish agony and poverty. The dark and murky karmic hindrances that make our lives miserable are the offerings that Buddha wishes to receive. His greatest won is for all sentient beings to cultivate their minds and achieve Buddhahood.

Never confront a karmic hindrance. The karmic hindrance is immense and as hard as rock, because you have practiced it for countless lifetimes, and you have not yet awakened the Dharma power. If you face it head on, you will break first, like an egg thrown at a rock. If you generate reverence, however, your karmic hindrances will simply melt away. Therefore, imagine that Sakyamuni Buddha is in front of you, and offer up your karmic hindrances with reverence. Even if you have to force yourself, surrender with reverence.

Even before you surrender, when a karmic hindrance begins to arise, believe that Buddha is in front of you and generate reverence with all your heart in order to offer up that mind. Before long, the karmic hindrance will disappear. Do not think "I" will eradicate this karmic hindrance, but simply surrender it with the truthful mind that turns to Lord Buddha. It will be like turning on a light switch in a dark room.

Praying for "my" success, and practicing the Dharma for the peace of "my" mind and to attain "my" enlightenment are all the practice of the ego.

In order to attain complete liberation and enlightenment, we have to offer up everything within us—the mind and the body, happiness and sorrow, distress and anxiety, and the Five Desires and Eight Sufferings[6]. Then, tranquility and Dharma bliss will fill the mind. This is the state of always being with Buddha. If you turn away from Buddha even for a moment, suffering and agony arise at once.

---

[6] The Buddha said there are eight sufferings in life: the suffering of birth, suffering of old age, suffering of sickness, suffering of death, suffering of separating from loved ones, suffering of associating with those we dislike, suffering due to unfulfilled wishes and desires, and suffering of the flourishing of the Five Skandhas (form, consciousness, feeling, perception, and formation).

The thing called "I" must cling to something. It cannot stand alone. This is why it is hard for sentient beings to escape from suffering and the cycle of rebirth. Once you offer up, or surrender, everything to Buddha, since there is no pride or ego remaining, there can also be no envy, jealousy, conflicts over recognition, or fighting over gain. It is the state of the Pure Land of Permanence, Bliss, True Self, and Purity, resplendent with reverence and joy.

Usually, people say "I will become enlightened," or "I will awaken to the Truth." Enlightenment becomes difficult with such an attitude. You have to remove the "I" to awaken to the Truth. The way to remove "I" is to do everything to please Buddha's mind. Yet, if there is no Buddha in your mind and you say "I will become enlightened," you will always be frustrated in your efforts, even after tens of thousands of years.

The monastery where practitioners follow the precepts faithfully, cultivate the mind well, and plant merit before Buddha—such a monastery is blessed with the grace and radiant energy of Buddha.

Observing the Precepts[7] is important. However, it is not good if your mind is constrained by them. If your mind is always turned to Buddha and enlightened sages, your speech and actions will naturally accord with the Precepts.

---

[7] The Precepts are a Buddhist code of ethics and morality, intended to help students avoid committing sins and planting the causes of negative karma. There are sets of Five, Eight, and Ten Precepts, and also a more detailed system of monastic rules for monks and nuns. The most basic are the Five Precepts: (1) to abstain from killing living creatures; (2) to abstain from taking what is not given; (3) to abstain from engaging in sexual misconduct; (4) to abstain from lying (5) to abstain from intoxicants.

If you surrender all your arising thoughts to Buddha by reciting Mireukjon Yeoraebul, Mireukjon Yeoraebul, Mireukjon Yeoraebul . . . on those thoughts, and diligently read the Diamond Sutra in the morning and the evening, then with the help of the mysterious bright energy, you will feel profoundly refreshed, and a renewed strength will arise within you. What else could this be but the grace of Buddha?

To cultivate the mind means to empty it. It is the practice of constantly emptying the mind of the three poisons—greed, anger, and ignorance, or deluded arrogance—through the practice of giving to others, surrendering the mind, and lowering ourselves. Rather than trying to be above others or defeat others, we should practice yielding to others, respecting others, and caring for others. Emptying and lowering oneself this way is called the cultivation of the mind.

There can be no wisdom where none has been cultivated. There can be no blessed fortune if none has been planted. Wisdom is a great inner wealth that enlightens our eternal lives, and merit is a blessed fortune that enriches our daily lives.

Because the state of one's mind depends on how one trains it, practicing constantly is important. If you practice the mindset of finding the faults of others, you will always be finding faults in others. If you practice a vengeful mind, the vengeful mind will continually arise. Once you start to discipline a child harshly, you end up treating the child harshly all the time. In the same way, if you persevere in practicing reverence, the mind will become truly reverent. If you practice reverence to your mind's fullest extent, your face also becomes radiant and pure like that of an innocent child.

Whatever you do, you should do it to serve Buddha. When you have a meal, meet someone or lose your mindfulness, at such moments you must practice the mind that you are doing these things to make Buddha happy. Buddha is the only place where karmic hindrance cannot exist. "Exerting the mind without attachment" is only possible when your mind is directed to Buddha. Without such a mindset, you turn to your karmic hindrances without even realizing it.

There is a saying that goes, "Do not stay where Buddha is, and run away from where there is no Buddha." Even with Buddha, enlightenment, and truth, if we cling to them with attachment, we only end up confining them in our narrow mind. When you can surrender the Buddha or enlightenment that your own mind has created and confined, will you then be able to perceive the true nature of Buddha, who radiantly fills the universe. Surrendering each and every thought is the path of a noble person.

Buddha said that we should adhere to neither the Dharma nor that which is not the Dharma. Having heard the Dharma, we should simply practice it.

Since wisdom, miraculous powers, and enlightenment all reside in the mind, do not seek for them outside the mind. The universe is in essence a peaceful place, but the minds of sentient beings are constantly seething with their own discriminative notions. A healthy mind is able to remain calm and wise in adversity or in prosperity. In Samadhi, tranquil like a deep lake, non-conceptual wisdom deepens and the true nature of the universe is revealed as on a mirror.

7. A Life's Purpose

The purpose of life should be to benefit others
while living brightly oneself
Thinking about what we can do for our country and
our surroundings is the path we should follow

The sentient being who is closest to you is not a family member, but your own body. This is because your spirit, not your body, is your true self. For countless eons, we have lived thinking that the body is the true self, and have pursued the Five Desires (desire for money, sex, food, fame, and sleep), while living as a slave to the body. When you turn to Buddha, you begin to live for your spirit.

Everyone who cultivates the mind wants to solve the problem of birth and death. However, we should serve Buddha with reverence before anything else. Trying to solve the problem of birth and death for one's own benefit is also the practice of ego.

There are many people who respect Buddha, but those who cultivate the mind are rare. No one looks forward to the strenuous practice of reading the sutra and surrendering for many hours. Nothing in this world is free, however. To move forward, you must pay your way, with effort and devotion. Furthermore, in order to improve, you must put whatever you have learned into practice. The spiritual path requires an attitude of devoting all your heart and soul to the task.

Very often we pursue spiritual practice to fulfill our wishes and for the sake of our bodies. However, cultivating the mind means to eradicate the ego of "I" and bodily attachment caused by the false notion of "I." Ask yourself what you can do for Buddha, what you can offer up to Buddha, and whether you can even generate such a mind. The Mind of the Great Vehicle is the mind that says, "Buddha, I will serve you brightly."

There is nothing that is not based on won. Since a heart-felt won invoked before Buddha will eventually become reality, the won should be made radiantly and broadly. Furthermore, we should not simply talk about an enlightened life, but put it into practice. The grandest and brightest won that we can invoke is the vow of serving Buddha. For every situation you encounter, pray "May this issue be resolved brightly to make Buddha happy, barwon." For every person you meet, "May this person awaken faith and devotion to Buddha, to serve Buddha well." Invoke a won that bright wisdom will arise, so that you can serve Buddha as brightly as the sun, and plant great merit. Even when looking at the sky and the trees, if you invoke wons that they may awaken faith and devotion to serve Buddha well and accumulate much merit, you free yourself from the ego of "I," and become part of the greater flow of serving Buddha. Thus your actions will automatically become Buddha's work.

Even though you live in the secular world, if you do not avoid the tasks or situations you encounter, but surrender to Buddha the thoughts and discriminative notions that arise in such situations and handle them with the mindset of serving Buddha, even the work of the secular world becomes the work of Buddha that benefits and enlightens many people.

In the Diamond Sutra it is written, "Tathagata [literally meaning "thus gone one," one of the common epithets of Buddha] knows and sees all sentient beings." The Tathagata is said to know and see not only the seven billion people who live on the earth, but also all the animals and plants. The Tathagata is aware of every thought of every sentient being. In other words, the Tathagata knows the thoughts that arise moment by moment, and all of our wandering minds. We exist within Buddha's radiance. Whether we are at work, driving on the road, or at home, Buddha knows and sees all.

It is a noble intention to practice Buddha's teachings in order to cultivate the mind or to cleanse karmic hindrances. A person who thinks this way is rare and precious. However, if you think to yourself that "I" will practice, or "I" will cleanse my karmic hindrances, it is difficult for you to progress. Hidden beneath your intention to pursue practice and become enlightened is your ego. In the Diamond Sutra, it is said that when you cleanse all your notion of "self" and "others," and the notion of sentient beings, you are simply Buddha. The shortcut to eradicating the self is to live your life in order to make Buddha happy, and to make serving Buddha's mind the purpose of your practice, as far as you are able.

Practitioners usually hope to advance in their practice to impress the people around them with their progress. With such a thought, one's practice will not go far. Spiritual practice is the process of cleansing one's karmic hindrances. If you let your mind become attached to the consequences of spiritual practice and to growing your own spiritual power, it is very dangerous. Practitioners usually believe that this is the correct way of thinking, but from an enlightened perspective, it is not correct. Nothing will be achieved in this way, even after many lifetimes of strenuous practice. Spiritual practice means a state where there is no "self," and where the ego of "I" has disappeared.

If you practice Buddha's teachings and cultivate the mind with the thought that "I" am pursuing the Dharma, "I" must become enlightened, and "I" must cleanse the karmic hindrances, your ego and the ego of those around you will clash, and the result will be suffering. However, if you can keep the practice schedule and surrender your mind in order to serve Buddha, everything will be much smoother. The world is innately tranquil. It is your own discriminations that make it turbulent and unsettled.

Even spiritual seekers will stray from the path when they begin to be attached to the "I." They become attached owing to the false belief that the "I" is a real thing, and end up losing all kinds of virtuous merit. The biggest thief in the world is karmic hindrance. Only those who constantly keep watch and are not be deceived by it will be able to protect their most precious treasures.

Spiritual practice means enlightening the soul by turning towards Buddha's radiance.

In the mind that is full of ego and karmic hindrance, although one may claim to have reached the non-discriminating state, it is only words and karmic hindrance. However, in the state of absolute reverence, there is no "I." Therefore, everything you do will become non-discriminating.

Do not spend your life chasing after worldly matters, but establish your principles firmly and keep them as the foundation of your life.

Thoroughly understanding the world, whilst not becoming attached to it—this is the way to realize the nature of greed and practice the Dharma in the secular world. By realizing the nature of greed, you can understand the principles behind economic activities. By cleansing yourself of anger, you can maintain peaceful and harmonious relationships with others. Thus, by cultivating your own mind, you can attain true principles and morality.

When you go to the monastery, go there with the intention to make Buddha happy. Everyone goes to the monastery for their own benefit, but if you can go to the monastery to please Buddha's mind, this is something rare and beautiful.

Even after a thousand lifetimes, you cannot escape the condition of a sentient being. Yet, if you can practice the thought that you want to make Buddha happy, even if it is not wholehearted, because such a thought rarely arises in the human mind, your karmic hindrances will be checked and your good roots will deepen.

Regardless of what you do, if you do it to make Buddha happy, this is the act of giving without attachment. As described in the Bible passage, "Blessed are the poor in mind, for theirs is the Kingdom of Heaven."[8] When the mind is free and without barriers, purified of ego and attachment, you become one with the universe, and accumulate virtuous merit without limit.

---

[8] In the Korean translation of the Bible, the word for *pneuma*, commonly translated as "heart or "spirit" in English, is *maeum*, the Korean word for "mind." *Maeum* is translated as "mind" in this passage and throughout this book.

Whatever you do, you should do it to serve Buddha. When you have a meal, or meet someone and lose your mindfulness, at such moments you must practice the mind that you are doing these things to make Buddha happy. Buddha is the only place where karmic hindrance cannot exist. "Exerting the mind without attachment" is only possible when your mind is devoted to Buddha in reverence. Without such a mindset, you turn to your karmic hindrances without even realizing it.

Do not think of reverence as an abstract concept. Instead, simply believe and see others as Buddha. If you do this, reverence arises and your mind is transformed.

Reverence is the state in which your mind falls into a realm of radiance. When it attains reverence, the mind is elevated to a new enlightened level.

Before you go to bed at night, reflect upon the day and how you spent it. Consider whether you said anything to bring hurt to others or did anything that caused harm to others. In order to make up for one or two bad deeds that day, you must perform three good deeds before you go to bed. Each day's outcome should be resolved on that day. If you did two bad deeds today and plan to perform three good deeds tomorrow, this is not the way to live a truthful life. Today's affairs must be settled today. The future of a person who can settle matters day by day is bright indeed. In our lifetime, how much greed, anger, and arrogance have we cleansed? How much merit have we planted before Buddha? Are we currently living honorable lives, so that we will not feel ashamed on our deathbed? The only things we take with us after death are the mind we have cultivated, the sins we have committed, and the merit we have planted. This stern Dharma lecture is one we should live with, engraved in our hearts.

The sickness of society stems from the decay of the spirit. From this decay come corrupt attitudes, toxic industrial fumes, sexual assaults, and environmental pollution. Who will inherit this polluted environment, however? It is we who will inherit it, when we are reincarnated in the next life. Karmic causality is not subject to the smallest error. One who causes much pollution will live surrounded by much pollution. Therefore, to free ourselves now from the causes of such consequences in the future, and to cure the corrupt spirit, we should generate the reverence of making Buddha happy, even though it is not our natural mindset. To take one more step towards a brighter realm, to escape the shackles of karmic hindrance and causality that keep us far from brightness, practice the Dharma with the thought that you want to please Buddha's mind.

The Buddha's Dharma is the practice of lowering and emptying oneself. In order to lower and empty ourselves, we have to serve the people around us as Buddhas. If we enshrine Buddha in our mind, our affairs cannot but go smoothly. If you reverently enshrine the fragrant radiance of Buddha in the mind, all your words and thoughts will be enlightening; you will have no misfortunes, and conflict with nothing. If a person speaks while clinging tightly to the "I," everything becomes a source of conflict. The ego's mind wave provokes the ego of others and the flame of conflict arises. Therefore, you must cleanse your ego. If you reverently enshrine Buddha in the mind, the twenty-four hours you live each day will be blissful indeed.

A spiritual practitioner should plant merit before Buddha without words, and resolve his or her problems wisely. While practicing the mind of working and living for Buddha, if a thought arises such as "What about myself?" you should notice that this is a karmic hindrance generated from ego, and immediately surrender the thought to Buddha.

The stronger the sense of "self," the more suffering and conflict you will face. When there is no self and one simply attends to the Buddha, radiance and happiness are all that remains. If you serve Buddha, your mind becomes peaceful, but if you serve the "I," life becomes difficult. When your mind is peaceful, your words and deeds are peaceful as well—for there is no ego of "I."

If a person invokes a won to serve Buddha, fragrant reverence will completely fill that person's body and mind. If one invokes a won to plant merit before Buddha and puts that won into practice, the person will receive the blessed fortune of that merit. An enlightened master invokes the won, "May all sentient beings be liberated from the karmic hindrances and retributive karmic ties that have accumulated over countless past ages, may they be freed from every misfortune, and fulfill their wishes to serve Buddha brightly, accumulating merit for every single life to come."

The universe is completely filled with the bright radiance of Buddha. People, however, cannot sense this radiance because of their karmic hindrances. The moment we see another person as Buddha, the karmic hindrance of the "I," or ego, subsides. At such moments, you can directly sense the radiance of the universe and become one with Buddha's energy.

To serve Buddha means to attend Buddha with reverence. The practice of cultivating the mind finally becomes radiant and complete when it is based on the mindset of serving Buddha.

In order to become one with Buddha, the "self" cannot exist. Where there is no "I," there is pure wisdom and enlightenment.

If you say, "I will comfort sentient beings and lead them to salvation," this is the mind of arrogance and great ego. Since your mind is directed not to Buddha but to sentient beings, you could easily imprint on your mind the karmic hindrances of sentient beings, and become like them. In order to perform the Bodhisattva Act, one must have at the foundation of one's mind the sincere wish and resolution to make Buddha happy. A person who surrenders the thought that he or she is performing good works, who surrenders even the virtuous merit that has been planted, and who humbly stands in the place of service to Buddha—is this not a true Bodhisattva? The task of saving sentient beings is Buddha's task, and our task is to serve Buddha.

Those who pursue spiritual practice are undoubtedly blessed with Buddha's grace. But if you become frustrated because the work you do for Buddha is overwhelming, then Buddha will also be uncomfortable.

Whether it is your spiritual practice or work, you must be wise enough to do it in accordance with your ability.

When you are experiencing great suffering, offer this prayer to Buddha, "May everyone be freed from such suffering so that they can awaken devotion to Buddha and plant much merit, barwon."

You should not view Buddha as a separate object of reverence and "I" as a separate being offering up reverence. Where there is absolute reverence, there is no "I" and there is nothing to be separated. Therefore, do not think of Buddha as a separate object, but simply bow down to the mind that reverently calls out "Lord Buddha" and continue your spiritual practice towards that mind, believing that you are in the presence of Buddha.

The scent of the reverent mind is thicker than that of fragrant fruits. A string that has been used to tie fish will smell like fish. A paper that has been used to wrap incense sticks will be sweet-scented. If the three poisons (greed, anger, arrogance) are the like the smell of fish, a kind and humble mind is like a fragrant scent. We should consider what scent we are giving out to our surroundings.

You can truly love yourself when you love your soul. Only when you love your soul can you love your country. To love one's country is to love the many people who belong to that country, and such is the attitude of the Bodhisattva Mind.

Practice with the mentality that you are actually in the presence of Buddha. Generate thoughts and perform deeds that will make Buddha happy.

If you are a practitioner, you should keep the precepts and purify your mind, so that you can convey to others the warm energy and virtue that you cultivate, and develop the ability to calm their sufferings. The purpose of life should be to benefit others while living brightly oneself. Thinking about what we can do for our country and our surroundings is the path we should follow.

Feeling superior or inferior to others and wanting to be well-treated by others is caused by one's arrogance and attachment to "I." The notion of "I" is attachment to the body and the source of all suffering. In the mind that reverently serves Buddha, there is no suffering from "I." Furthermore, because "I" is not permitted in the service of Buddha, in that moment, everything is heavenly and enlightening.

See others as Buddha. A wife should see her husband as Buddha, and a husband should see his wife as Buddha. See your colleagues at work as Buddha, and see your neighbors as Buddha. In such moments, Buddha's radiance and compassion, which fills the mind, will put us at ease and melt away the deeply-ingrained karmic hindrances of past lives. The bliss and reverence you feel at the moment you see others as Buddha is greater than any wealth or sensual pleasure that life can offer. A person who can enjoy such inner bliss and gently smile is one who practices the Bodhisattva Mind, the Bodhisattva Act, and the Bodhisattva Path.

Spiritual practice should be undertaken on the basis of absolute reverence to Buddha. Our mind must be one of reverently folding our hands and bowing down upon hearing even the name of Buddha.

Avoiding all sin, performing good deeds, and purifying one's mind—such is the teaching of all the Awakened Ones.

– Dhammapada (Verses of Dharma)

By offering up all of your profit, greed, and fame to discipline the mind, by gladly devoting and sacrificing yourself for many people, you cultivate the Bodhisattva Path.

A mind filled with the joy of the constant practice of good deeds and planting virtuous merit—this is a life of true happiness.

Words of Wisdom
from enlightened masters

Appreciation for the good must be long-lasting;
Hatred for the wicked must be passing and brief

−King Sejong the Great

- **The Caigentan** (Vegetable Root Discourse)

When the wind has passed through a grove of bamboo trees, the rattle of the stalks dies away. After the wild geese are gone, their reflection in the deep pool disappears. Likewise, for a noble person, things come up and, when they are gone, the mind is empty once again. (Book I. 82)

Do not blame others for trifling transgressions; do not reveal the secrets of others; do not bear in mind the long-past misdeeds of others. Cultivate these three virtues and you will keep away from harm. (Book I. 105)

Try to cover up the faults of others. If you speak badly of others, it is like attacking one fault with another. If people are stubborn, guide them well so that they can see their errors. If you feel hate and anger, it is like trying to cure stubbornness with stubbornness. (Book I. 121)

I should tolerate the excesses and mistakes of others without objection, but never my own. I should put up with my own humiliation and disgrace, but never that of others. (Book I. 168)

When things do not turn out as you wish, think of those less fortunate than you. Your grievances will vanish without effort. When the mind grows lazy, think of those who are better than you. Your spirit will be effortlessly renewed. (Book I. 215)

• Master Wonhyo (617~686 AD)

When sewing garments, a tiny needle is sufficient, and a long spear is useless. When sheltering from rain, a small umbrella is sufficient, and one that covers the entire sky is needless. Never dismiss the things that appear to be of no consequence. Whether small or large, anything can be a precious treasure depending on its nature.

Hotness is the nature of the sun; coldness is the nature of the moon. If there were only sun, and no moon, the seeds would burn and wither, and none would bear fruit. If there were only moon, and no sun, the seeds would rot away, and none would sprout.

There are those who, having learned but a little, vigorously defend their own limited viewpoint. They are pleased with others who share their opinion, and scorn those who disagree. Such is like a person looking at the sky through a reed stalk. They praise others who also look through a reed, and claim that those who do not cannot perceive the sky. This kind of ignorance criticizes the wise—and while having little wisdom, believes that it is great.

One who realizes that he is in delusion is not greatly deluded, and one realizes that he is in darkness is not in total darkness.

To have faith means to truly believe in the existence of the Dharma, to believe that it can be attained through the practice, and that when one attains it through practice, it brings boundless virtue and merit.

- **King Sejong the Great (1397~1450)**

Appreciation for the good must be long-lasting; Hatred for the wicked must be passing and brief.

(Sejong Sillok, 19 April, 1425)

If you approach a task with pride and arrogance, you cannot achieve it; if you approach a task with humility and sincerity, you can definitely achieve it.

(Sejong Sillok, 8 December, 1427)

When the Heavens nourish the earth, they do not distinguish between the great and the small. When a king loves his people, it should be the same.

(Sejong Sillok, 14 May, 1439)

● **Dhammapada** (Verses of Dharma)

Hatred is never solved by hatred.
Only by calming the hatred does it end.
This is an ancient truth. (5)

Long is the night to one who is awake.
Long is the mile to one who is tired.
Long is samsara [the repeated cycle of life and death]
to the foolish ones, ignorant of true Dharma. (60)

This is an old saying, O Atula, not only of today:
They blame him who sits in silence,
They blame him who speaks a lot,
They blame him who speaks little,

There is no one on earth who is not blamed.
There never was, never will be, nor is now,
A man who is only blamed, or a man who is only
praised. (227-228)

As rust arising from iron corrodes the very iron from
which it arose, so do transgressions lead their doer to
a state of woe. (240)

One is not wise only because one speaks a lot.
One who is peaceful, without hate, and fearless, is
said to be wise. (258)

If, by giving up lesser joys,
One could experience greater happiness,
A wise person would renounce the lesser
To behold the greater. (290)

The offering of Dharma surpasses all offerings,
The taste of Dharma surpasses all savour.
Delight in Dharma surpasses all delights.
The destruction of craving conquers all suffering. (354)

If you spend your day amid good deeds,

Blessed fortune may not follow instantly,

But harm will keep away.

If you use a day for wicked deeds,

Harm may not immediately befall you,

But fortune will keep away.

Like the grass that grows on a hill in springtime,

Those who do good deeds may flourish unnoticed.

But day by day, in some wise they do grow.

As the whetstone grinds the knife,

Those who do evil may not seem to weaken,

But day by day, in some wise they decline. (Chapter 1)

If you sow rice, you shall reap it.

If you plant beans, they will grow.

The net of the heavens is cast so wide,

That though unseen, none can escape it. (Chapter 2)

Fortune abounds in an honest and thrifty house,

Virtue blooms amid modesty and humility.

Enlightenment comes where there is peace and tranquility,

And in beings where there is warmth and radiance.

Greed begets ill-fortune

Disasters lie in wait for those who covet.

Carelessness and pride beget error,

And where there is no kindness, there will be sin.

Guard your eyes, lest you see faults in others.

Guard your mouth, lest you speak of others' flaws.

Guard your mind against greed and anger.

Guard your body, and fall not into bad company.

(Chapter 5)

Having served, expect no reward; having given, have no regret. (Chapter 7)

Though you own a broad mansion of ten thousand feet,
you need only a space of eight feet to sleep at night.
While your rich fields may be twenty thousand acres,
two bowlfuls of rice is all one needs for a day.

(Chapter 12)

If you wish others to think highly of you,
there is no better way than to think highly of others.

(Chapter 17)

The luster of youth does not return
No day has a second dawn.
Devote yourself to learning when you are young,
For time waits for no man. (Chapter 25)

The green mountains tell me to live without words
The clear sky tells me to live without wrongs.

"Leave love behind, leave hatred behind,
Like the water, like the wind"
Thus do they tell me to live, before I depart.

The green mountains tell me to live without words,
The clear sky tells me to live without wrongs.

"Leaving anger behind, leaving greed behind,
Like the water, like the wind"
Thus do they tell me to live, before I depart.

Cultivating the Mind: A Path toward Enlightenment

Written by Kim, Jae Woong

Translated from Korean

First edition March, 2014

Yong Hwa Publications
1269 Seonggok-ri, Heunghae-eup, Pohang
Phone: 054-261-2231

Diamond Sutra Recitation Group NY
158-16 46th Ave. Flushing, NY 11358
Phone: 718-539-9108
Email: kbgdtny@gmail.com

ISBN 978-89-969357-7-3 02220 :

Printed in the Republic of Korea

People always try to put themselves higher, but the water always finds the lowest place. The stream lowers itself to become a river, and the river lowers itself even further until it cannot go any lower and reaches the sea.

p. 159

In this monastery full of pure energy, devoting my life to making Buddha happy along with young spiritual seekers, who come with selfless ideals, and receiving warm spring rays with them is indeed the truest happiness. It is said that the spiritual practitioner's chest and the green forest in the early morning give out life energy. The reason why this monastery has become more radiant and peaceful is because of Buddha's white radiance and the power of the spiritual seekers' practice. A life without greed, a life of cleansing karmic hindrances, a life of illuminating wisdom, a life of planting merit before Buddha—this is the life of pure happiness.

p. 241

Without practice, the realizations that one has are no more than a useless theory, and they will never become part of us. Only those who put their realizations into practice can harvest the fruits of their study.

p. 261

• Dharma Master **Kim Jae Woong**

Polishing the Diamond
Enlightening the Mind

369 pages
Also available as an eBook

"**D**espite wanting happiness and wishing to avoid suffering, human beings constantly engage in activities that give rise to fear, disease, starvation, and ultimately death. Under such circumstances it would be wonderful if even a few people could create some inner peace, if only for a short time. I am confident that readers who seek such a goal will find valuable advice in this book." —*H.H. the Dalai Lama*

"**M**aster Jae Woong Kim offers the reader instructions, delightful allegorical tales, and moving stories about his own master. Based on his understanding of the Diamond Sutra, Master Kim uses these stories to point to the profundity of ultimate wisdom and compassion." —*Tricycle: The Buddhist Review*